History of Australia and Aboriginal Mythology

An Enthralling Journey Through the Australian Past and the Legends of Its First Peoples

© Copyright 2025 - All rights reserved.

The content contained within this book may not be reproduced, duplicated, or transmitted without direct written permission from the author or the publisher.

Under no circumstances will any blame or legal responsibility be held against the publisher, or author, for any damages, reparation, or monetary loss due to the information contained within this book, either directly or indirectly.

Legal Notice:

This book is copyright protected. It is only for personal use. You cannot amend, distribute, sell, use, quote, or paraphrase any part, or the content within this book, without the consent of the author or publisher.

Disclaimer Notice:

Please note the information contained within this document is for educational and entertainment purposes only. All effort has been executed to present accurate, up-to-date, reliable, and complete information. No warranties of any kind are declared or implied. Readers acknowledge that the author is not engaging in the rendering of legal, financial, medical, or professional advice. The content within this book has been derived from various sources. Please consult a licensed professional before attempting any techniques outlined in this book.

By reading this document, the reader agrees that under no circumstances is the author responsible for any losses, direct or indirect, that are incurred as a result of the use of the information contained within this document, including, but not limited to, errors, omissions, or inaccuracies.

Free limited time bonus

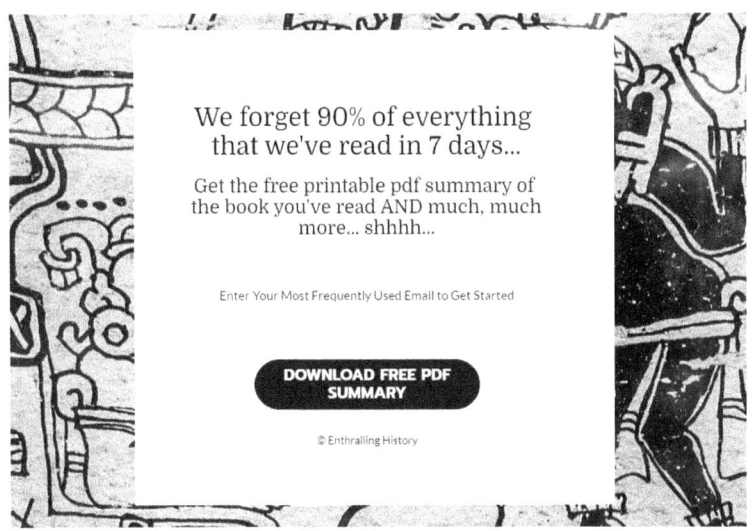

    Stop for a moment. We have a free bonus set up for you. The problem is this: we forget 90% of everything that we read after 7 days. Crazy fact, right? Here's the solution: we've created a printable, 1-page pdf summary for this book that you're reading now. All you have to do to get your free pdf summary is to go to the following website:

https://livetolearn.lpages.co/enthrallinghistory/

Or, Scan the QR code!

Once you do, it will be intuitive. Enjoy, and thank you!

Table of Contents

PART 1: HISTORY OF AUSTRALIA 1
    INTRODUCTION: AUSTRALIA—A COUNTRY THAT IS AS UNIQUE AS A PLATYPUS BEAK 3
    CHAPTER 1: BEFORE AUSTRALIA WAS AUSTRALIA—INDIGENOUS ORIGINS 5
    CHAPTER 2: DISCOVERY AND EXPLORATION: EUROPEAN ARRIVAL IN AUSTRALIA 13
    CHAPTER 3: COLONIZATION AND CONVICTS: THE FOUNDING OF BRITISH SETTLEMENTS 22
    CHAPTER 4: GOLD RUSH AND ECONOMIC BOOM: THE TRANSFORMATIVE 19TH CENTURY 36
    CHAPTER 5: THE PUSH INLAND, FEDERATION, AND THE BIRTH OF AUSTRALIA 42
    CHAPTER 6: WORLD WAR I AND AUSTRALIA'S INCREASING ROLE IN GLOBAL CONFLICTS 53
    CHAPTER 7: THE INTERWAR PERIOD, ABORIGINAL RIGHTS, AND A STOLEN GENERATION 60
    CHAPTER 8: AUSTRALIA DURING WORLD WAR II 64
    CHAPTER 9: IMMIGRATION, REVITALIZATION, AND THE SHAPING OF MODERN AUSTRALIA 73
    CHAPTER 10: THE ECONOMY AND ENVIRONMENTAL AND POLITICAL CHALLENGES 79
    CONCLUSION: AUSTRALIA'S FUTURE FOREIGN POLICY 91

- PART 2: ABORIGINAL MYTHOLOGY 93
  - INTRODUCTION 95
  - CHAPTER 1: DREAMTIME CREATION MYTHS 97
  - CHAPTER 2: SONGLINES AND THEIR SPIRITUAL SIGNIFICANCE 103
  - CHAPTER 3: THE LORE OF THE RAINBOW SERPENT 110
  - CHAPTER 4: ABORIGINAL CONSTELLATIONS AND CELESTIAL MYTHS 116
  - CHAPTER 5: TOTEMIC BONDS: ANIMALS AND ANCESTORS 125
  - CHAPTER 6: BOOMERANGS: MORE THAN JUST A PIECE OF WOOD 136
  - CHAPTER 7: ETHICS AND MORALITY IN ABORIGINAL LEGENDS 144
  - CHAPTER 8: DEATH, REBIRTH, AND THE AFTERLIFE 153
  - CHAPTER 9: NATURE AND ITS LINK TO ABORIGINAL MYTH 159
  - CHAPTER 10: SPIRITS OF THE OUTBACK 167
  - CHAPTER 11: ABORIGINAL WARRIORS WHO FOUGHT FOR THEIR LANDS 176
  - CONCLUSION 186
- HERE'S ANOTHER BOOK BY ENTHRALLING HISTORY THAT YOU MIGHT LIKE 188
- FREE LIMITED TIME BONUS 189
- FURTHER READING AND REFERENCE 190
- IMAGE SOURCES 193

Part 1: History of Australia

An Enthralling Journey through the Ancient Indigenous Cultures, European Settlement, Colonial Era, and Modern Times

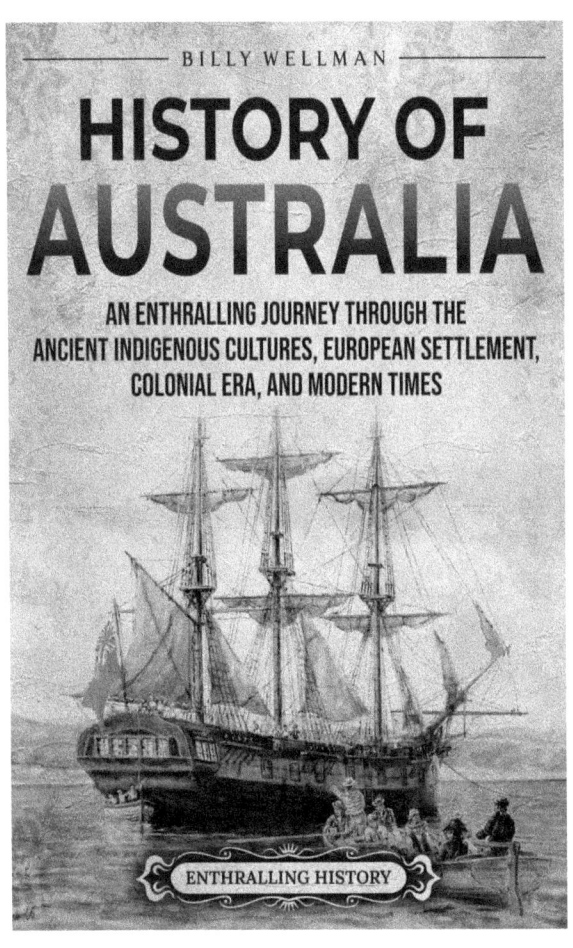

Introduction: Australia—A Country That Is as Unique as a Platypus Beak

Perhaps it is the understatement of the century, but Australia has a rather unique history. Australia is also a rather unique place. This continent has some of the rarest flora and fauna on the planet. After all, Australia is home to a warm-blooded mammal that lays eggs. Everywhere else, that is strictly the business of reptiles and birds, but just try to tell that to the platypus!

The platypus is a marsupial. This critter is closely related to the porcupine, but it still has many unique features. Besides laying eggs, this animal carries a deadly venom. Throughout most of the world, animals like scorpions, spiders, and snakes carry venom. In Australia, a cute and cuddly platypus packs a deadly venomous punch. However, it would be more accurate to say kick in the case of the platypus. The hind legs of the animal produce the venom, and it is injected into its victim through special spurs on its back feet.

This animal is so strange, with its fur, duck-styled beak, beaver tail, reptile-like crawl, and otter-like feet, that many early biologists who were given dead specimens to examine insisted that the bodies had to have been fake. These esteemed scientists were absolutely certain that this Frankenstein beast just could not be real. They insisted that it must have been stitched together from the parts of several other creatures.

There is no other way to put it: this part of the world is one of a kind. This was one of the main draws for early European explorers. They wanted to learn more about this strange region. As time passed, Europeans settled in the area.

Captain Arthur Phillip, the man who is, in many ways, considered the founder of modern Australia, is certainly a polarizing figure. He planted a flag in Sydney Harbor in 1788, beginning widespread settlement of the region. Some hail him as a hero, while others decry him as a usurper who appropriated the lands of others.

Nevertheless, whether we love him or hate him, it is hard to deny his bold audacity. He sailed very far from his home and was determined to make do in (what was to them) an entirely alien land.

Phillip did this by choice. It is important to note that many others were brought to this strange land not by choice. For many years, convicted criminals were sent to Australia as punishment. Australia has had more than its fair share of sarcastic remarks about how it got its start as a penal colony, but such things are simply a part of Australian history.

The convicts might have initially been brought to this land against their will, but they learned to survive in this new terrain. Some of them even escaped the clutches of their taskmasters long enough to become so-called "bushrangers." These rough and tumble rebels, for all of their faults, are yet another strand in the fabric that makes up the Australian tapestry. From the real-life Ned Kelly to the fictional Crocodile Dundee, the notion of rugged individualists roughing it in the bush and making their own rules is the stuff of legend.

Yes, just like the platypus, Australia is the whole of many unique parts that seem to, impossibly enough, somehow complement each other despite being diametrically opposed.

Chapter 1: Before Australia Was Australia—Indigenous Origins

"This is what my father taught me and this is what I have to teach my sons, and my son has to teach his sons the same way as my father taught me. And that's the way it will go on from grandparents to sons, and follow that jukurrpa. No one knows when it will end."

-Paddy Japaljarri[1]

About ten thousand years ago, the world was still firmly in an ice age. This was a geologic period in which much of the world's surface was either covered with ice or decidedly cooler than it is today. Even places that would be considered beachfront property now might have been rather chilly at times during this epoch.

We have to use the term "beaches" loosely because back in the Ice Age, the modern eye likely would not recognize much of the terrain of what we now refer to as Australia. The sea levels were much lower back then since much of the ocean water was frozen in glaciers. These low sea levels created land bridges between areas that would later be filled with all of that melted ice water.

The most famous example of this is the Bering land bridge, located between North America and Eurasia. It is full of water now, but when the water levels were lower, it is strongly believed that a land bridge linked

---

[1] Macintyre, Stuart. A Concise History of Australia. 1999. Pg. 10.

these two continents. Essentially, it would have been possible for a person to walk from Siberia to Alaska across this dry stretch of land. It has been theorized that this was how Native Americans first arrived in the Americas.

When it comes to Australia, there were a few land bridges that were of great importance. There was the Bassian Plain, which linked Australia to Tasmania, and there was the Sahul, which joined Australia to New Guinea. Both created corridors that would have allowed ancient Australians to travel overland to reach new regions to settle and explore.

In fact, it is believed that Australia was still connected to New Guinea by the Sahul land bridge as recently as eight thousand years ago.[2] That might seem like a long time ago, but in the long human history of Australia (which some say goes back at least sixty-five thousand years ago), it would be more like yesterday.[3]

Scholars believe these low water levels and land bridges facilitated the first migrations to the landmass we now call Australia. The waters between Asia and Australia were much narrower, and island chains were much closer. Because of this, it is thought that the earliest people to arrive in Australia did so by navigating across these island chains in canoes.

Even the simplest of canoes could have sailed the short distances between islands until one reached Australia proper. This is backed up by many Indigenous legends that have been passed down countless generations. These tales speak of long treks across the water by canoe for various reasons and purposes.

The traditional way of life of the Indigenous people of Australia, better known as the Aboriginal people, has its own unique set of positive and negative aspects. There is no such thing as a perfect society; all cultures have what might be perceived as good virtues, as well as customs and cultural behaviors that might be perceived as bad. Of course, what constitutes good and bad is usually based on the perceptions of an outside, dominating culture.

Let's look at an example. Some of the Aboriginals of New Guinea, just north of the Australian continent, are said to have engaged in cannibalism. There is still some debate on this matter, but most scholars agree that cannibalism was indeed practiced at some point in New Guinea's history,

---

[2] Macintyre, Stuart. A Concise History of Australia. 1999. Pg. 15.
[3] Macintyre, Stuart. A Concise History of Australia. 1999. Pg. 9.

something that none other than US President Joe Biden seemed to agree with.

Biden was visiting a war memorial site in Pennsylvania when his speech took a surprising turn. In a random offhand anecdote, he suggested that his uncle had been eaten by cannibals when he crashed his plane in New Guinea. Biden's uncle was a pilot during World War II, and he became marooned in a part of New Guinea. He was never heard from again.

Of course, the fact that such a thing was alluded to does not make them true, and it most certainly does not make them any less controversial. Shortly after Biden spoke those words, there was an immediate backlash. Even the prime minister of Papua New Guinea, James Marape, weighed in on the controversy. Prime Minister Marape stated that these misconceptions about Papua New Guinea were wrong and hurtful and should be avoided.

While Biden's remark became a point of controversy, it highlights a broader issue: long-standing Western misconceptions about Indigenous cultures in the Pacific region. For centuries, colonial narratives and sensationalized accounts have shaped how certain societies have been perceived. Early explorers and anthropologists often exaggerated or misunderstood Indigenous practices, sometimes portraying entire communities in a negative or exoticized light.

At any rate, it is safe to say that most of us today would frown upon any cultural practice that involves eating people. As far as we know, no Indigenous tribe practices cannibalism today. Such things are not seen as an acceptable cultural trait by the vast majority of the world now, any more than it was considered acceptable hundreds of years ago.

It is believed that only a small portion of the Aboriginal people actually engaged in cannibalism. It has become somewhat of a norm to paint Indigenous people with the same brush. However, we have to understand that the Aboriginals were made up of many diverse tribes that all had their own unique cultures. One tribe might have practiced cannibalism, and another tribe might have been horrified by it.

All cultural perceptions aside, the Aboriginal people of Australia can certainly be proud of the fact that their ancestors were even able to find their way to Australia in the first place. It is believed that the first Aboriginal people arrived in Australia around sixty thousand years ago. The Aboriginal people are one of the oldest continuous cultures on Earth.

The first Aboriginal people arrived during the last Ice Age. Australia was a lot different back then. When these newcomers arrived in this strange new land, they had to find a means to eke out a sustainable existence. The first people of Australia had to be smart and able to think on their feet. After all, they were encountering what was basically a new world of unknown flora and fauna.

Although the later European explorers often get a lot of credit for their daring missions over the high seas to get to Australia, this should not diminish the bravery of the earliest Australian explorers. They also faced a new and alien world. Upon reaching Australia, they encountered incredible species of animals, some of which no longer exist. They might have encountered a giant variation of the kangaroo that is said to have been nearly three meters (almost ten feet) tall. They also likely encountered the now-extinct *Diprotodon*, which was a relative of the wombat and the size of a modern-day rhinoceros.[4]

The Aboriginals likely sampled the local plants and animals with caution at first, but over time, they became accustomed to the resources this island continent had to offer. For example, the *Diprotodon* became a favorite target of hunters. In fact, the large marsupial, which went extinct some twenty-five thousand years ago, is believed to have been overhunted by the Aboriginals, similar to how the Native Americans are thought to have brought about the end of the giant sloth in North America. The giant sloth of North America and the *Diprotodon* of Australia did not have much defense against human hunters. So, when bands of humans showed up and began mercilessly cornering the beasts and making them a regular food source, they were most likely driven to extinction as a result.

The fact that the emergence of humans in a new, untouched environment led to the extinction of animals is not surprising. As author and historian Geoffrey Blainey put it, the arrival of humans "into new regions is usually accompanied by the extinction of species."[5]

The Aboriginals were not known to store food, so their population level is not believed to have been very high. Storing food is a necessary step for sustaining a larger population. Otherwise, groups of humans are limited by the resources that can be hunted or gathered at the time.

---

[4] Blainey, Geoffrey. *A Shorter History of Australia.* 1994. Pg. 6.
[5] Blainey, Geoffrey. *A Shorter History of Australia.* 1994. Pg. 6.

Another facet of Aboriginal life that is often missed by many historians is the impact of tribal warfare. Some might feel inclined to depict the ancient Aboriginal people as peaceful, but this is not an accurate depiction. It defies both the common history of humanity and its general push toward violence, as well as the history of the Aboriginals in particular.

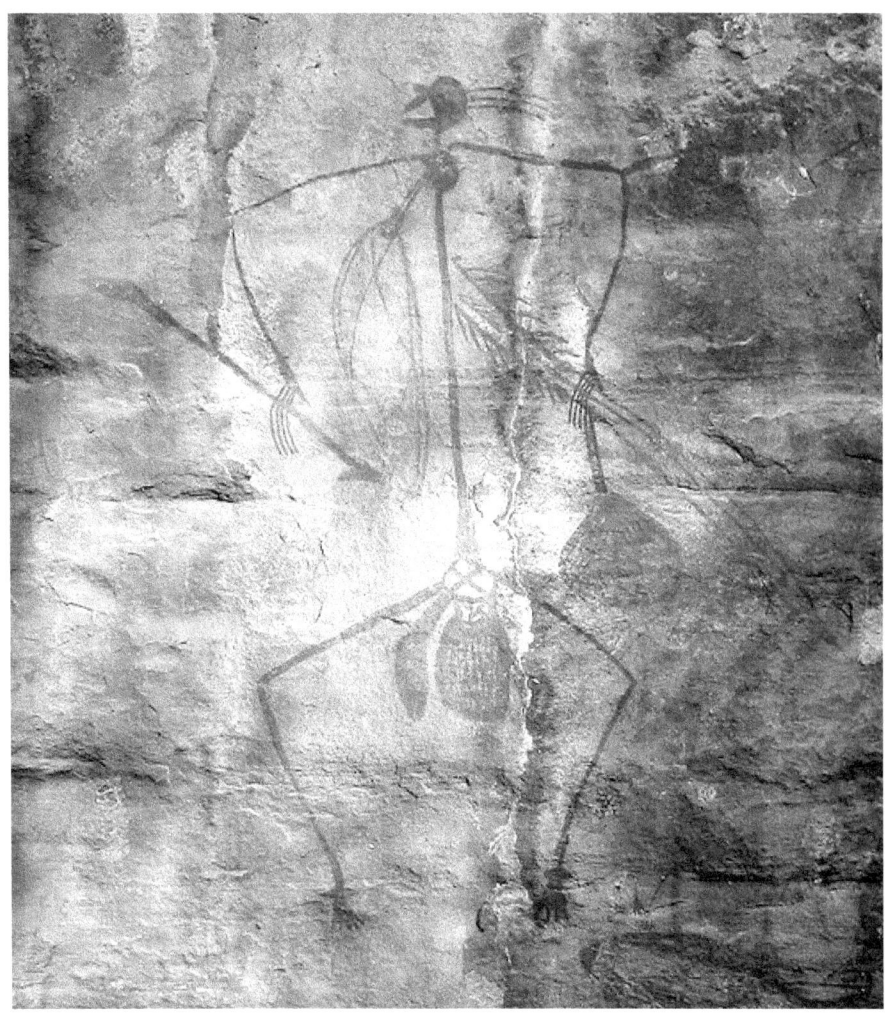

Aboriginal rock art.[1]

It has long been known that vengeance killing among the Aboriginals was common. Sometimes, superstitious beliefs led to massacres. If a person perished from some terrible disease or illness, one could ascribe the death to evil spirits. They could even say that those evil spirits had been summoned by a tribal enemy. Of course, such beliefs defy the logic of most of us today, but this was a common practice among the Aboriginals in the past. If one group seriously believed that another group had utilized spirits to kill one of their tribe, it could trigger an all-out war between the two tribal groups.

A spate of intertribal warfare was documented by outside sources as late as 1875. During that year, a great massacre took place in central Australia among the Aboriginals, which is said to have left nearly one hundred dead and many more injured.[6] No one seems to know what started this conflict, but it could have been sparked by a perceived slight. These episodes of violence would have also served to curb the population growth among the Aboriginals of Australia.

As it pertains to the overall population of the ancient Aboriginals, some scholars have floated numbers like one million, but such a thing seems doubtful. Most scholars peg the peak population of Aboriginals to be closer to 500,000 at most. It is estimated that this is likely the maximum number of people that could be sustained on a hunter-gatherer lifestyle in Australia.

The term "hunter-gatherer" can be viewed as both a term of historical significance for humanity as a whole, as well as a vocation of the Aboriginals in particular. It is believed that all of humanity went through a hunter-gatherer stage at some point. It was only when civilizations began to settle down and plant crops that farming replaced hunting and gathering as the main source of food. The rise of farming allowed for more controlled resources and more complex versions of societies.

Rather than living out in the bush chasing any rabbit they saw, people were able to establish long-term settlements where all of their needs were readily provided for them. This also established a firm hierarchy, in which some were categorized as being of a higher rank than others. These distinctions left a mark.

When Europeans encountered the Aboriginals centuries later, they tended to look down on them as being part of the lowest rung of society. The roots of their subsequent prejudice can be found here.

The European explorers believed those they encountered were destined to adopt their ways and leave behind what they considered the primitive backwaters of a hunter-gatherer civilization. But what many of

---

[6] Blainey, Geoffrey. *A Shorter History of Australia*. 1994. Pg. 10.

these first European explorers failed to realize was that the hunter-gatherer lifestyle of the Aboriginals had become perfectly balanced and adapted to the environment in which they lived.

Later anthropologists would come to see this prejudiced misconception as being rather flawed in light of the fact that the Aboriginals lived just fine within the confines of their hunter-gatherer society for tens of thousands of years.[7]

It has been estimated that the average lifespan of an Aboriginal was likely fifty years. This was due to a wide variety of reasons, such as illness, environmental factors, and violence.

In regard to environmental factors, the mighty El Niño effect likely created a lot of the environmental hardships that Indigenous Australians faced. El Niño induced droughts, which left the eastern two-thirds of the continent periodically parched. These long droughts likely made the Indigenous people conclude long ago that sedentary farming was not a practical means of sustenance in their harsh environment.[8]

Despite these environmental challenges, the Aboriginals proved to be tenacious and ingenious as it pertained to how they handled these difficulties. The Aboriginal people were always on the move. A mother with young children would have found mobility a bit difficult. Yet, someone, somewhere along the way, must have looked at the kangaroo hopping around with a baby in its pouch and gotten an idea. The Aboriginals began to take kangaroo skins to fashion their own makeshift kangaroo pouches, which women would put over their backs so that they could walk while carrying their babies with ease.[9]

It is believed that these early residents utilized the native gum trees for kindling. These early Australians sat around campfires, which they used to keep warm and for lighting. As the indigenous peoples of Australia sat around these campfires, they were able to lean back and wonder. Like any human on the planet who is given ample time to think about themselves and their condition, philosophical notions began to come to mind.

The Aboriginal people began to ask deep and meaningful questions. "Who are we? How did we get here?" they mused to themselves. In order

---

[7] Macintyre, Stuart. A Concise History of Australia. 1999. Pg. 13.
[8] Macintyre, Stuart. A Concise History of Australia. 1999. Pg. 15.
[9] Blainey, Geoffrey. *A Shorter History of Australia*. 1994. Pg. 7.

to answer these puzzling questions, they began to develop their own personal belief systems.

Today, anthropologists would likely refer to these as creation myths. However, it is important to realize that for the people who developed these beliefs, they were not myths at all.

While these beliefs might sound strange to outsiders, they made sense to Native Australians. In fact, many Native people of Australia still believe in the Aboriginal concept of the Dreaming. Now, to be clear, we are not speaking about those strange snippets of the subconscious mind we experience when we lay down to sleep in our beds. Instead, the Dreaming refers to an ancient and ongoing spiritual belief that the world was created through the dreams and actions of supernatural beings. Their dreamy thoughts carved out rivers and pushed up mountains. Their dreams conceived of plants and animals of all kinds, including human beings. Aboriginal belief contends that since we are all made of this same basic dream essence, there is a certain mutability as it pertains to everything else that exists. There is a belief that one form of life and existence can merge and blend with another. Even so, honoring one's ancestors and what came before is considered crucially important.[10]

In Stuart Macintyre's book, *A Concise History of Australia,* an Aboriginal elder by the name of Paddy Japaljarri Stewart describes a kind of "dream maintenance" that Aboriginal believers feel compelled (perhaps even responsible) in maintaining, lest the dream should end, and their culture and tradition fade away.

---

[10] Macintyre, Stuart. A Concise History of Australia. 1999. Pg. 9.

Chapter 2: Discovery and Exploration: European Arrival in Australia

"From what I have said of the Natives of New Holland, they may appear to some to be the most wretched people upon the Earth, but in reality, they are far more happier than we Europeans; being wholly unacquainted not only with the superfluous but the necessary Conveniences so much sought after in Europe, they are happy in not knowing the use of them. They live in a Tranquility which is not disturb'd by the inequality of condition; the Earth and sea of their own accord furnishes them with all things necessary for life."

-*Captain James Cook*[11]

We have to be very careful when we speak of the "discovery" of Australia. We have to recognize that the island had already been discovered by other groups of people before the Europeans arrived. We must realize that when we speak of discovery in these terms, we are more specifically speaking of the Europeans' discovery.

There is actually some debate over which European power first discovered Australia. It has long been suggested that the Dutch held this honor, although some have suggested that it was the Portuguese. The

---

[11] Macintyre, Stuart. A Concise History of Australia. 1999. Pg. 28.

debate over whether it was the Dutch or the Portuguese who first stumbled onto Australia is understandable considering how competitive these two European powers were at the time.

The Portuguese were the first to round the tip of South Africa; they achieved this milestone in 1488. This opened a new route to India, as they could circumnavigate around the tip of South Africa and then head northeast through the Indian Ocean. This kickstarted a push for further European exploration of India and other parts of the world that had previously been hard to reach. The Dutch were close on the heels of the Portuguese and explored many of the same regions that the Portuguese did.

Some say that the Portuguese from their southeastern Asian island outpost of Timor, where they established a base in 1516, occasionally had ships driven off-course. They perhaps caught sight of the northwestern coast of Australia as a result.[12] If so, they did not attempt to do much to pursue that mysterious coastline.

In 1605, Portuguese explorer Pedro Fernández de Quirós, sailing under the Spanish Crown, led an expedition in search of the great southern land (Terra Australis), a vast, semi-mythical continent that many Europeans believed lay hidden in the Southern Hemisphere. Convinced that they were on the brink of discovering this uncharted territory, the Spaniards envisioned it as a new land ready for exploration, bestowing upon it the grand title Australia del Espíritu Santo ("Southern Land of the Holy Spirit").

When Quirós reached the New Hebrides (modern-day Vanuatu), he named the largest island La Austrialia del Espíritu Santo, intentionally modifying the spelling to honor King Philip III of Spain, who belonged to the House of Austria. Believing he had finally set foot on the legendary southern continent, Quirós announced his discovery with great enthusiasm. However, in reality, he had only reached an island, falling short of the vast landmass he had hoped to find.

As far as we know, it was the Dutch who etched the first reliable record of Australia into history. In 1606, a ship under the command of the Dutch East India Company (VOC), called the *Duyfken*, a name that translates roughly as "Little Dove," became the first known European vessel to make landfall on the Australian mainland.

---

[12] Blainey, Geoffrey. *A Shorter History of Australia*. 1994. Pg. 23.

The *Duyfken* was captained by Willem Janszoon, who, along with his crew, charted approximately 320 kilometers (200 miles) of coastline along the Cape York Peninsula (modern-day Queensland). At the time, they mistakenly believed they were exploring part of New Guinea, not a new continent. Janszoon's voyage also marked the first recorded European encounter with Indigenous Australians, including a hostile skirmish that resulted in casualties among his crew.

While Janszoon's maps were limited, his landing in 1606 remains a milestone in European exploration, predating James Cook's famous 1770 voyage by more than 160 years.

Later that year, a former deputy of Pedro Fernandes de Queirós, Luís Vaz de Torres, made his way toward Australia along the Torres Strait (which was subsequently named after him) from New Guinea. Although Torres laid sight on the Australian mainland, he most likely did not realize just how expansive the land was.

Still, it was the Dutch who led the charge as it pertained to mapping out Australia. A Dutch explorer named Dirk Hartog initially ended up doing so by accident. In 1616, he found himself off course after rounding the Cape of Good Hope en route to Batavia. Back in those days, Batavia was the capital of the Dutch East Indies. It would later become the Indonesian capital, Jakarta.

At any rate, this crew that launched off from Batavia found itself landing near the western portion of Australia's coastline known as Shark Bay. It must be stressed that they landed near Australia and not on it. They actually landed on a nearby island. However, Australia was within sight, and it would not be long until many more landings would be made.

In 1622 (some say 1623), a ship called the *Leeuwin*—Dutch for "Lioness"—set anchor on the southwestern coast of Australia. Though few records of this voyage remain, it is believed that the crew charted parts of the coastline in what is now Western Australia. The headland they encountered would later be named Cape Leeuwin in honor of this fateful journey. Unlike other Dutch expeditions that focused on the northern and western coasts, this voyage marked one of the earliest European encounters with Australia's southwestern region.

A few years later, in 1627, another Dutch navigator, François Thijssen, took exploration a step further. Sailing aboard the *Gulden Zeepaert* ("Golden Seahorse"), Thijssen became the first European to chart much of Australia's southern coast. He and his crew mapped over 1,800 kilometers (1,100 miles) of coastline, revealing a landmass stretching far beyond what was previously thought.

In the following year, 1628, a whole Dutch squadron was sent by the governor-general of the Dutch East Indies himself, Pieter de Carpentier. This expedition was tasked with taking a look at the continent's northern coastline. Many great discoveries were made during this particular expedition, including the discovery and subsequent naming of the Gulf of Carpentaria.

As you may have already guessed, this gulf was named after Pieter de Carpentier. Yes, everyone was quite eager to literally make a name for themselves as they discovered or commissioned new expeditions to new and extraordinary lands that had never been seen by European eyes before. It also must be noted that though these voyages expanded the Dutch understanding of the region, the Dutch never attempted to settle the land. Instead, their discoveries laid the groundwork for later explorers.

European explorers also paid attention to the surrounding region. One of the most significant figures in this effort was Abel Tasman. In 1642, sailing under the flag of the Dutch East India Company (VOC), Tasman set out on an expedition to further explore the unknown lands beyond the Indies.

Abel Tasman.[2]

Later that year, Tasman and his crew became the first Europeans to lay eyes on the landmass we now call Tasmania—an island off the southern coast of Australia. He named it Van Diemen's Land after Antonio van Diemen, the governor-general of the Dutch East Indies. Pushing farther east, Tasman went on to become the first known European to reach New Zealand, though his attempt to land there ended in conflict with the Māori, resulting in the deaths of several of his men.

Tasman never actually sighted the Australian mainland, but his voyage was still groundbreaking. He helped solidify the Dutch understanding of the southern lands, and his maps later played a role in shaping European knowledge of the region. Tasman became the first to call Australia by the name New Holland. Decades later, Dutch cartographers would apply the name New Holland to Australia, cementing the legacy of the Dutch in the early mapping of the continent.

In fact, these efforts led to the near-complete mapping of most of Australia and the surrounding region by 1648. This map was put together by a Dutch mapmaker named Joan Blaeu and was dubbed the "Nova et Accuratissima Totius Terrarum Orbis Tabula."

The British were not about to let the Dutch have all the glory, and in 1688, a British explorer—and part-time pirate—William Dampier, made his way to Australia's northwest coast. Dampier was serving aboard the *Cygnet*, a ship full of privateers-turned-pirates who had spent the past few years plundering Spanish territories and raiding vessels across the Pacific. Unlike the Dutch explorers who had mapped Australia with official backing, Dampier and his crew arrived by accident, looking for a quiet place to repair their ship.

After sailing through Indonesia, they made landfall near King Sound (modern-day Western Australia). Dampier became one of the first Englishmen to step foot on Australian soil. While his visit was not part of an official British effort to claim Australia, it marked the beginning of British interest in the continent. A decade later, Dampier returned—this time, not as a pirate, but as a government-backed explorer.

William Dampier took it upon himself to document the land and its inhabitants in great detail. In 1703, he published his book, *A Voyage to New Holland*, in which he recounted his experiences exploring the northwestern coast of Australia. Dampier's descriptions of the land were vivid. He noted the barren, dry landscapes, the strange flora, and the unfamiliar wildlife, including large hopping creatures that would later be recognized as kangaroos (this word originates from the Guugu Yimithirr word *gangurru*).

More notably, Dampier was also among the first Europeans to write about the Indigenous Australians. He described them as "the miserablest people in the world," commenting on their lack of clothing, houses, and European-style agriculture. From his European perspective, he saw their nomadic lifestyle as a sign of poverty rather than an adaptation to their environment. He remarked on their dark skin, curly hair, and thin physiques, noting that they seemed to survive primarily by fishing and foraging. Though Dampier acknowledged their skill in hunting and their use of spears, his harsh and dismissive descriptions reflected the biases of his time.

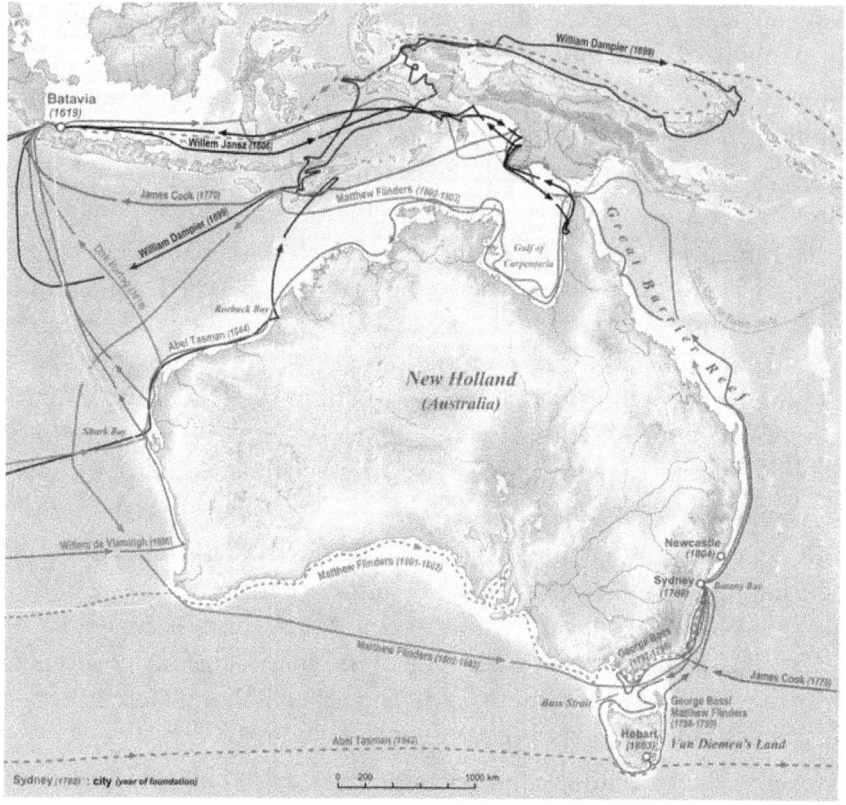

Voyages of European explorers before 1813.[8]

The later voyages of Englishman James Cook built upon much of what Dampier and others had discovered. James Cook was in the British navy and was the captain of the HMS *Endeavor*. In 1769, he and his crew embarked upon a mission to Tahiti, supposedly to take note of the transit of Venus as the planet traversed across the sky.

This was not the first time that Cook had been involved in observing astronomical events. In 1766, he had been part of a team that documented a solar eclipse, the transit of which had been viewed over Newfoundland in North America.

The task of documenting the transit of Venus from Tahiti was officially commissioned by Britain's esteemed scientific body, the Royal Society. Oxford scholar and professional botanist Joseph Banks tagged along with the crew. The observation of the transit of Venus was a milestone of great importance for science since the distance between the Earth and the sun could be made using these observations for the first time in history.[13]

There was, however, an ulterior motive at work. Along with charting the course of Venus, Cook had secret orders to see if he could reach Australia and perhaps make a claim on the land for the British.

The British had been largely shut out of Australia by this point. Since other European powers had already sunk their teeth into the continent, Cook had to be very discreet about how he undertook his exploration/conquest of Australia.

On April 19th, 1770, Captain James Cook and his men spied land off the southeastern coast of Australia at a place he later named Point Hicks. They continued sailing northward and, on April 28th, 1770, entered a large bay where the landscape was described by Cook as "as fine a meadow as ever was seen." The bay was initially called Stingray Bay, but after botanists Joseph Banks and Daniel Solander collected an astonishing variety of plants, it was renamed Botany Bay.

Cook then embarked on a harrowing journey up the northeastern coast, charting the land and making periodic landfalls. At times, his men carved marks into trees to leave signs of their journey. However, the expedition nearly ended in disaster on June 11th, 1770. Cook's ship, the *Endeavour*, struck a coral reef—part of what is now known as the Great Barrier Reef. The ship took on water, but after a desperate struggle, Cook and his crew managed to beach and repair it at Endeavour River, where they remained for seven weeks.

Despite the challenges, Cook pressed onward. On August 22nd, 1770, he landed on Possession Island in the Torres Strait, where he formally claimed the entire eastern coast of Australia for Britain, naming it New South Wales. His voyage would later set the stage for British colonization, forever changing the course of Australia's history.

Interestingly, Cook's earliest observations of the region were glowingly positive, with little inclination of the hardships that later explorers would face. Unbeknownst to Cook, he had landed in the middle of what was Australia's rainy season. This was a time when the soil would appear much more fertile than during the dry season, and water, in the form of flowing streams, would be present.

---

[13] Blainey, Geoffrey. *A Shorter History of Australia*. 1994. Pg. 25.

James Cook marveled at what he thought was rich and robust grasslands. He suggested that the grasslands were so great that cattle could graze there all year round. Considering his glowing description, later explorers who arrived in the land during the dry season were shocked to find a parched hellscape with little resemblance to anything like what James Cook had described.[14]

Captain James Cook.'

Britain had its hands full at the time. Its colonies in North America were on the verge of a full-out rebellion. These thirteen colonies would soon declare war against Britain.

---

[14] Blainey, Geoffrey. *A Shorter History of Australia*. 1994. Pg. 25.

Against all odds, the upstart colonists won the war, forming the United States of America and forcing the British to admit defeat in 1783. After Britain lost most of its territory along the Atlantic coast of North America, it began to take a serious look at Australia. Britain's Home Office issued a document in 1786 that established Botany Bay as a site for potential settlement. This document also outlined the grand scheme of transforming Australia's Botany Bay into a penal colony, a decision that would have ramifications for many generations to come.[15]

Why this particular spot was chosen is still debated. It could be that it was simply the most well-trod spot on the coast by the British at this point in time. It has also been argued that the British felt the region put them in a strategically advantageous position as it pertained to the Dutch East Indies, which was located nearby. It is also argued that the location had plenty of much-needed resources, such as flax, timber, and even whales. Others, however, contend that the British merely wanted to send their undesirables as far away as possible.

This is, of course, a rather simplistic and cynical view, but its premise is a logical one, albeit based on hindsight since we know that Britain would indeed send many prisoners to Australia.

---

[15] Macintyre, Stuart. A Concise History of Australia. 1999. Pg. 28.

Chapter 3: Colonization and Convicts: The Founding of British Settlements

"The truth is, of course, that my own people, the Riratjungi, are descended from the great Djankawa who came from the island of Baralku, far across the sea. Our spirits return to Baralku when we die. Djankawa came in his canoe with his two sisters, following the morning star which guided them to the shores of Yelangbara on the eastern coast of Arnhem Land. They walked far across the country following the rain clouds. When they wanted water they plunged their digging stick into the ground and fresh water followed. From them we learnt the names of all the creatures on the land and they taught us all our Law."

-*Wandjuk Marika*[16]

Although some historians insist that the portrayal of Australia's founding as a penal colony is somewhat overblown, there is still plenty of truth to be found in such assertions. Numerous convicts did indeed arrive to live in the early settlement located near Australia's Port Jackson.

The port had been established in Sydney Harbor and was named after Sir George Jackson, who had served as the lord commissioner of the British Admiralty. This port eventually became the staging grounds of a

---

[16] Macintyre, Stuart. A Concise History of Australia. 1999. Pg. 9.

grand experiment in forced labor and settlement.

Those who had been convicted of crimes back home in Britain, which included prostitution, theft, and even murder, were sentenced to exile in Australia. Once they arrived, they would be forced to help build what would later become a bustling colony.

Their legacy has lasting repercussions that can be felt to this very day. A sizeable number of modern-day Australians descended from convicts, and many of these descendants are actually quite famous. For instance, former Prime Minister Kevin Rudd is descended from a colonial convict.

In 1788, Britain's First Fleet arrived on Australian shores in force. Captain Arthur Phillip was established as the governor-general of the fledgling colony. Arthur Phillip and company had left Britain in May 1787 with eleven ships. On board these vessels were sailors, convicts, marines, and officers. All of them were forced to live in cramped quarters for the duration of the trip.

A portrait of Arthur Phillip.[5]

The journey from Britain to Australia was, of course, quite an adventure, and along the way, the First Fleet made several important stops. Their first stop was at the Canary Islands (Tenerife), where they rested for a week before continuing southwestward to Rio de Janeiro, Brazil. There, the fleet docked for about a month, allowing the crew to rest, repair ships, and resupply before setting sail once more.

After departing Brazil, Governor Arthur Phillip and his crew took a southeasterly course to the tip of South Africa, where they docked at Cape Town for another month. These were all foreign-controlled ports, and as such, the British had to tread carefully. Although they had nothing to fear from the Portuguese authorities in Brazil or the Dutch in South Africa, they were still guests in these lands and had to respect local rules. Britain's biggest rival at the time was France, but even in neutral ports, Phillip made sure his men remained disciplined to avoid any trouble that might delay their historic journey.

After spending a month in Cape Town, Arthur Phillip and his fleet sailed off. The First Fleet finally reached its destination at Botany Bay some eight months after it first departed from British territory. The fleet carried around 443 naval personnel, 759 convicts, and 160 or so marines, the latter of whom were tasked with keeping the convicts in line.

As you may suspect, the prisoners did not have much say in the matter, but many of them were led to believe they were being taken to a veritable paradise, a land of great bounty. Furthermore, they had been promised that in exchange for working and tilling the fields, they would eventually secure their own freedom.

Of course, this idyllic picture was far from what these souls actually experienced upon their arrival in January 1788. Australia was not the paradise that had been described, and their existence would be a hard one. Initially, every day was a struggle just to keep going.

The First Fleet set anchor during the region's harshest season, right in the midst of a scorching summer. The absence of rainfall had turned the ground into a dry, scorching hellscape. Clean water was very difficult to come by, so all the resources had to be carefully rationed among the settlers.

Nevertheless, on January 26th, 1788, British flags were raised over the port that became part of a new settlement called Sydney. It was named in honor of British Secretary of State Lord Sydney. This day—simply known as Australia Day— has since been heralded as the moment that modern Australia was founded. However, for those whose ancestors already lived in the region before the British arrived to settle the land, this day would come to be known as Invasion Day. In their eyes, this was the day that a foreign force took hold of their ancestral lands and changed the lives of those who dwelled there forever.

The first real change the Aboriginals faced came in the form of diseases spread by the newcomers. These settlers—whether they realized it or not—carried pathogens that the isolated Aboriginal people had never encountered. Their immune systems had no defense against these viruses. Of all the pestilences that were brought to Australia, the dreaded disease known as smallpox was the worst. Smallpox is believed to have decimated at least half of the local population in a very short time after its introduction. Some estimates state around 80 percent of the Aboriginal population was killed by European diseases. According to historian and scholar Barbara West, the disease took only a matter of months to lay waste to these Indigenous Australian communities.

As much as the Aboriginals suffered, it would be both wrong and perhaps a disservice to paint them as merely defenseless spectators to the arrival of the British. On the contrary, they were active participants, and there were times they decided to strike back against those who had dared to occupy their land. At one point, Governor-General Arthur Phillip was ambushed by some locals and had a spear hurled into his shoulder. It has been said that Phillip ran for cover with the spear still protruding from his arm. Fortunately for him, it was just a flesh wound, and the injury did not become infected.

A depiction of the Aboriginals from 1784.[6]

Despite being injured like this, Phillip—unlike what many others might have done—refused to take any retaliatory action. He seemed to realize that what had happened to him was likely a (rather painful) misunderstanding and did not want to escalate the situation any further. This is a sign of smart leadership, as one should be able to pick and choose their battles.

Phillip eventually achieved some rather promising relations with the locals. Interestingly enough, the fact that he was missing one of his teeth actually aided him in this regard. It was an Aboriginal tradition for older, more esteemed members of the tribe to yank one of their front teeth out. It was seen as a special rite of passage.

So, when it was noticed that Phillip was missing a tooth, the Aboriginals saw it as a sign that he was an elder. He was seen as someone who was somewhat familiar with their culture and traditions. It was an ironic coincidence, but it managed to help smooth over relations that otherwise might have been much more difficult.

The Aboriginals were more than willing to show their teeth to the British. The British, of course, had the Aboriginals outgunned, so the Aboriginals did not have the capacity to launch a major offensive against them. As such, their attempts to push back against the colonizers took the shape of intermittent ambushes, such as the one Governor-General Arthur Phillip experienced.

Besides the threat of these occasional acts of violence, by far the most challenging aspect of these early settlers' lives was making sure they did not starve to death. The British brought a lot of supplies with them, but these supplies would only last for so long. Additionally, the supply ships did not always make it to Australia. For example, the British supply ship HMS *Guardian* set out from South Africa's Cape of Good Hope, only to find itself off-course in the southern seas. It slammed into an iceberg.

The loss of the HMS *Guardian* meant that extra food and supplies would not be arriving anytime soon. This meant that the Second Fleet would have to make do with what they already had, and the people would also have to do what they could to start growing their own crops once they reached land.[17]

---

[17] West, Barbara A. *A Brief History of Australia*. 2010. Pg. 42.

In June of 1790, the British Second Fleet made its way to Port Jackson with some rudimentary supplies and 733 more prisoners.

Due to the lack of enough supplies to go around for all of these newcomers, it became imperative to find ways to cultivate the lands of Australia. In an effort to further this cause, important farming tools were imported, such as plows, hoes, shovels, axes, and the like. This hardened prisoner workforce was handed these tools and expected to do the back-breaking labor of cutting away foliage, digging up the soil, and planting crops.

One of the first major setbacks they faced was a bad batch of seeds. The convicts had planted seeds for crops, but when they did not seem to take root, the British cast a wary eye toward the Dutch traders whom they had purchased them from. These seeds had been bought from the Dutch at the Cape of Good Hope and then brought to Australia. The British wondered if their sometimes rival, the Dutch, had purposefully sabotaged the seeds. Such things are possible, but it is also possible that Australia's harsh and often challenging environment was the culprit.

The rationing of food became even more severe as the colony struggled to survive. To prevent food supplies from being pilfered, Governor Arthur Phillip implemented harsh laws, making theft of rations a capital offense. Though this might seem extreme, one must consider the dire circumstances—the colony's food supply was dangerously low, and without strict rationing, everyone would have starved. Several convicts were executed for stealing food, as even a small theft could mean weeks of hunger for others.

In November 1788, the British established Parramatta, located farther inland from Sydney, in an attempt to find better farmland. Like Sydney, Parramatta began as a penal settlement, but it was intended to serve as an agricultural hub to support the struggling colony. However, both settlements faced severe shortages, and tensions ran high. Many of the convicts had been transported for theft, and in a colony where food was more valuable than gold, some were willing to risk their lives to steal it.

Along with the threat that they faced from within, the convict settlers also had to deal with an outside threat. Most of the interactions with the Aboriginals were initially few and far between. But as the settlers began to set down permanent roots, the clashes became more frequent. The biggest eruption of tensions occurred in 1790 in an incident known as Pemulwuy's War.

The war is named after an Aboriginal man who was seen as the spiritual leader of the conflict. Chief Pemulwuy is thought to have been around forty years of age when the conflict erupted. Pemulwuy and his band of warriors waged what was essentially a guerilla war against the settlers. Those who dared to set foot in the colony had to do so while constantly looking over their shoulder. This was especially the case if they ventured too far from the main settlements. Pemulwuy and his warriors were very familiar with the terrain, so they had an advantage in the fight.

This outbreak of fighting only came to an end in 1802 after Pemulwuy was shot to death. Demonstrating how much of a nemesis he was to the settlers, those who killed him made sure to cut off his head so they could send it back to their colonial taskmasters as proof that the chief was indeed dead.

A Scene of South Australia depicting German immigrants interacting with Aboriginals.[7]

In the midst of all of this fighting, colonial life continued. Farms and homesteads were maintained. During this period, livestock became a great boon to the settlers of Australia.

By 1795, nearly seven hundred sheep were dispersed among several farms near Sydney and Parramatta, marking the beginning of Australia's sheep farming industry. Just a few years later, by 1799, the colony's sheep population had grown to an estimated 4,588. Most of these early sheep were imported from South Africa's Cape Colony, but they were mainly used for meat rather than wool production.

Transporting livestock across such vast distances was incredibly costly and difficult, as settlers had to battle what historian Geoffrey Blainey later called the "tyranny of distance." With Australia being a remote outpost of the British Empire, supplies from Europe or even South Africa took months to arrive. Settlers had to make the most of the land available, focusing their farms along the fertile river valleys and coastal plains near Sydney, Parramatta, and the Hawkesbury River.[18]

In 1797, the colony took a major step toward becoming a wool-producing powerhouse when Merino sheep, originally from Spain, were introduced via South Africa. These sheep, prized for their fine wool, would lay the foundation for Australia's future as a world leader in wool production.

The cultivation of land was not the only thing that was encouraged. People were strongly encouraged to raise families. Marriage was made a top priority among both convicts and free settlers, as the colony needed a stable population to survive.

For most convicts, however, being sent to Australia meant permanent separation from their families. While many had wives and children back in Britain, they were not automatically entitled to have them sent over. Convicts were expected to serve their time alone, and many never saw their loved ones again.

That said, over time, some well-behaved convicts who had earned their freedom or received a "ticket of leave" were allowed to petition the government to bring their wives and children to Australia. This practice became more common under Governor Lachlan Macquarie in the 1810s as the colony shifted toward a free-settler economy. By the 1830s and 1840s, government-assisted migration schemes also helped bring over wives and children of former convicts.

---

[18] West, Barbara A. *A Brief History of Australia*. 2010. Pg. 10.

Though reunification was possible for a fortunate few, for many transported convicts, the price of their crimes was not just exile but the loss of their families as well.

The British realized marriage was important for the settlement of the colony for a wide variety of reasons. For one thing, a family structure provided stability and incentive for those who labored in the harsh Australian terrain to continue to work hard. They would not only work for their harsh British taskmasters but also for their own families, who depended upon their support.

Religion was also viewed as a fundamental pillar of the society that was being built, although unlike in previous colonial exercises, the exact type of religion that was to be embraced was left fairly vague. Britain had faced many years of tumult between Protestants and Catholics and even infighting between different Protestant denominations. In Australia, the settlers practiced many different Christian faiths. Initially, most settlers were Protestant, but in 1791, a massive influx of Irish Catholic convicts arrived. The Irish are said to have made up the largest group of established immigrants to Australia, with the exception of the English themselves, until the outbreak of World War I in 1914.

Many of these Irish prisoners had been convicted of the same sort of crimes as the other forced laborers in Australia, but there were some who had been convicted of a different sort of crime. They had been convicted of political crimes. Ireland had long been struggling against British rule, and many would-be revolutionaries were imprisoned. Some of these political prisoners inevitably found themselves in Australia.

However, it must be made clear that not all settlers were convicts during this period. As early as 1793, free settlers started to arrive in Australia. They arrived in fairly small numbers at first, but they would increase over time. These free settlers and the military officers stationed in Australia would forge a new class. These settlers and officers seemed naturally dispositioned to lord it over the rest.

This class of perceived elites was known as the Exclusives. The convicts were, by the nature of their conviction, made subservient to this free Australian class. Even after they had served the duration of their sentence, they and their offspring still had the sting of their previous poor reputation.

The arrival of a new governor-general—Lachlan Macquarie— in 1810 changed all of this. Macquarie was a no-nonsense lieutenant colonel who sought to establish law and order in light of previous unrest among military officers, the most notable of which was the Rum Rebellion, which shook up the whole colony in 1808.

On January 26th, 1808, on what was the twentieth anniversary of the settlement of Australia, Major George Johnston, who was in charge of the New South Wales Corps, headed a group of some four hundred troops in an attempt to overthrow the colonial government. These rebels managed to storm into the compound where Governor William Bligh was holed up and placed him under their custody.

William Bligh.⁸

This all-out mutiny had erupted after Governor Bligh banned the bartering of rum for food or wages. Prior to Bligh's ultimatum, rum had been used among the settlers as a form of currency. It was believed that this free-flowing alcohol was corrupting free and convict settlers alike. In a move to ensure discipline, Bligh forbade the practice.

By this point, most of the settlers already had a bad opinion of Bligh. He was viewed as being way too heavy-handed, and this last draconian command was seen as the last straw. So, Bligh was not just overruled; he was overthrown. The rebellion would be short-lived, though. Once the British Crown heard about it, the troops were forced to disband, and Major Johnston was arrested. Bligh found himself out of a job. He was ultimately replaced by Lachlan Macquarie as governor.

Macquarie not only sought to instill a greater sense of law and order; he also sought to make sure that this sense of law and order was applied to everyone evenly. Macquarie was not given to favoritism and openly embraced the full rehabilitation of the convict classes in the colony that he governed. He still used convict labor, though, as was evident in the major projects that established towns such as Bathurst and Penrith. Even so, Macquarie provided these workers with some kind of light at the end of the tunnel. He even paved the way for emancipated convicts to be given the right to purchase land of their own.

As one might imagine, the Exclusive class did not necessarily appreciate these inroads made by the former convicts. Still, Macquarie's tenure as governor seems to have been a stunning success. Under Macquarie, the colony expanded both territorially and economically. Governor-General Macquarie kickstarted huge public works projects, which built up colonial infrastructure. Notable buildings and bridges were built, and roads spiraled out from the growing capital of Sydney to the surrounding satellite settlements.

During Macquarie's time as governor, the population greatly increased. At the start of his administration, the population was around 11,590, and it is believed to have been around 38,778 toward the end of his tenure. These efforts would lead to Macquarie later being hailed as the Father of Australia.

However, this supposed founding father was not always popular with his peers, and the Exclusives, in particular, did not appreciate Macquarie's methods. His outreach to former convicts had the more affluent Australians, led by John Thomas Bigge, calling for his removal, which led to his dismissal in 1821. Macquarie was replaced by Sir Thomas Brisbane, who served as the sixth governor-general of New South Wales.

During Brisbane's time as governor, the settlements in Australia were given full colonial status, which came with all of the rights the British Crown granted to lands with such status. Additionally, the island of

Tasmania during this period was, for the first time, recognized as its own separate territory. It was now seen as being separate from the mainland.

Brisbane embarked on a decidedly less tolerant approach to the Aboriginals. His aggressive push against the local inhabitants would soon be keenly felt by them. This was especially true as it pertained to Tasmania, for in 1825, Brisbane launched the Black War.

This war was nothing short of an effort to push an entire ethnicity (hence the reference to "black" Aboriginals) from their ancestral lands. Brisbane established a clear dividing line between the colonial settlements and the Natives of Tasmania and then continued to push this line farther and farther south. Eventually, the Aboriginals of Tasmania were pushed off the island and relocated to nearby Flinders Island, which was established as a reservation for them. Despite all of these efforts, modern Tasmanian residents cite Aboriginal heritage, demonstrating that some remained and even intermarried with colonialists. It is believed that just over 5 percent of the Tasmanian population today identify as being of Aboriginal descent.

Although the main tactic was blatant aggression against the Aboriginal people, there were some people who took a much softer approach. Captain George Grey, who was operating out of western Australia in 1840, came to view the Aboriginals rather fondly. Even though the Aboriginals did not adhere to what was then considered modern society at the time, he felt they were very smart and quick-witted. He also considered the possibilities of what could be accomplished if colonists worked with these intelligent and capable people instead of working against them.

Captain George Grey and others like him embarked on efforts to supposedly "civilize" the Aboriginal people so they could be more readily absorbed into the rest of colonial society. It was believed that the biggest hurdle behind good relations between settlers and Aboriginals was the fact that Aboriginals lived a very unsettled life. They were wandering nomads and hunter-gatherers by nature, so it was believed that if they were taught to settle down in one place and learn how to farm, colonial society could more easily relate to them.

Getting the Aboriginal people to settle on one stable plot of land was the first step. But they also had to get the Aboriginals to wear Western-styled clothes, learn how to read and write, and convert to Christianity.

This was the dream that many of these more soft-hearted colonialists had. Many today would condemn the motivations and aspirations of these so-called "civilizers." However, these colonizers obviously felt that they were serving a good cause. Unlike those who aggressively brushed the Indigenous people aside, these people were making an effort to integrate the Aboriginal people into colonial society so there could be peace.

One of those who sincerely believed in these efforts of social, cultural, and religious conversion was Reverend Robert Cartwright, who served as a chaplain in the colony in 1820. Cartwright was later quoted to have said of this social experiment that the locals would "be completely weaned from [their] roving habits."[19]

Children were seen as the number one targets of this indoctrination. It was believed that teaching the younger generations was crucial for creating any real and meaningful change in Aboriginal society. It was thought that if the children could be taught and raised in Western ways, they would then teach their parents. Even more importantly, they would teach the generations after them, creating a lasting generational shift among the Indigenous population.

This decision to make a comprehensive outreach to youngsters would essentially lead to efforts to systematically brainwash Aboriginal children. In some cases, kids would practically be kidnapped to live at private institutions set up specifically for the task of indoctrinating them. The memory of this forced indoctrination would lead to lasting scars on later generations of the Aboriginal people of Australia.

The efforts indeed led to a generational and cultural shift, just not exactly the kind that those who perpetuated it had sought. The vacuum left by these stolen generations is one of the saddest legacies and lingering effects of colonization in Australia.

The efforts to educate Aboriginals in Western ways were fleeting at best. Some children did take to the education that was provided, but they were few in number. Most Aboriginal children ran from the school and were never seen again. In other words, there was no consistency in these efforts, so no real progress was made.

However, the depredations and encroachment on tribal lands were consistent and steadily eroded away what was left of the Aboriginal way of life. Most pressing was the growing number of sheep farms. As mentioned earlier, once the colonists got the hang of what type of sheep to use and

---

[19] Blainey, Geoffrey. *A Shorter History of Australia*. 1994. Pg. 43.

how to raise them, sheep farming became a very profitable business in Australia. By the mid-19th century, sheep farms had grown exponentially. These farmers took up a lot of land, and much of that land was the traditional hunting grounds of the Aboriginals. The Aboriginals were no longer able to hunt and gather on their own as they had in the past, so they became increasingly dependent on the colonists. They depended on handouts of supplies, such as flour, sugar, and the like, and worked odd jobs for colonial taskmasters. There was indeed a generational shift in the works for Aboriginal society and their traditional ways of life, but it certainly did not seem to be one for the better.

Chapter 4: Gold Rush and Economic Boom: The Transformative 19th Century

"Land where gaunt and haggard women live alone and work like men. Till their husbands, gone a-droving, will return to them again."
-*Henry Lawson*[20]

Since at least the early 1800s, gold had been known to exist in various parts of the Australian colony of New South Wales. In 1815, inmates consigned to building the Great Western Road discovered many small gold deposits. Additional discoveries of gold deposits were made in the 1820s and 1830s.

However, all of these finds were in small quantities. Even so, the locations were largely kept quiet by those in charge, just in case they might produce better results later on.

The real breakthrough moment for Australia's gold rush is actually related to the gold rush in the US territory of California in 1849. (The gold rush of 1849 would later lend its name to an NFL football team, the San Francisco 49ers.) The California Gold Rush is a classic tale of fortune, greed, and opportunity. But what does it have to do with Australia? The connection lies in a British-Australian transplant who spent some time in

---

[20] Macintyre, Stuart. A Concise History of Australia. 1999. Pg. 98.

California during the gold rush of 1849. His name was Edward Hargraves, and he was marginally successful in mining gold in California.

His real "eureka" moment came when he realized that the lands in California that contained gold looked strikingly similar to the land he had seen in New South Wales. Hargraves returned to Australia in January of 1851 and teamed up with another gold prospector, John Lister. Together, they forged a prodigious prospecting operation, which managed to strike gold in a location called Lewis Ponds Creek.

A painting of Hargraves.[9]

The expedition broke down when terrible infighting took place over just who would take credit for the finds. Some scholars have since argued that Hargraves and Lister's role in the gold rush was overblown, but shortly after their efforts began, a motivation to find gold in Australia seemed to take hold. It has been estimated that during the rest of the 1850s, Australian mining managed to dredge up some one thousand tons of gold. This new influx of gold made up around 40 percent of the global total production of the precious metal before the decade was out.

This gold boom went hand in hand with a population boom, with the Australian population reaching one million for the first time in the year 1861.

As one might imagine, the gold rush brought about some rather far-reaching socioeconomic changes. The most obvious change was the population's rapid transition from farming communities to mining towns. Due to this rapid shift, the previously booming wheat production of the Australian colonies fell considerably. In Victoria alone, it is believed that production dropped by 75 percent in the first couple of years of the gold rush. Sheep were left untended, and farms went unplowed as the average Australian sought to make it rich digging gold rather than digging ditches. As a direct result, the price of food went through the roof. Wheat products, potatoes, cabbage, and eggs became exceedingly expensive.

The very last ship of convict settlers, the Hougoumont, arrived in Western Australia on January 9th, 1868. This marked the official end of Britain's practice of transporting criminals to Australia, closing a chapter that had lasted eighty years. By this time, free settlers had come to outnumber convicts and their descendants, as waves of gold miners and immigrants had poured into the continent during the mid-19th century.

Most former convicts, whose sentences had long since been completed, quietly lived out their lives in settlements across Australia. It is likely that some even lived into the early 20th century, with writer and historian Geoffrey Blainey suggesting that a few hardy souls may have still been alive at the outbreak of World War II in 1939. While no official records confirm this, it remains an intriguing possibility, though many ex-convicts were reluctant to speak of their past due to the stigma.

It is also quite likely that some of these former convicts took to the goldfields, seeking fortune and a fresh start during the gold rush era of the 1850s and 1860s.

The mining towns and the towns near gold mines were rapidly overwhelmed by wave after wave of gold-seeking migrants. It was not likely that anyone was checking the backgrounds of these gold miners to see who had past convictions. Ironically enough, many of these gold miners had already tried their luck in California, only to become discouraged by what was perceived as the lawless nature of the gold mines and mining towns. According to historian and scholar Barbara West, these intrepid souls had flocked to Australia in order to take advantage of its well-established British laws and customs.

Not everyone benefited from these so-called British customs, though. Many miners arrived from China, and they had a rough go of things, especially when compared to their mining counterparts. Eventually, laws were even passed to restrict Chinese involvement in mining. Heavy taxes were levied against ships carrying Chinese migrants. Some Chinese found a way around this by showing up far from the goldfields in southern Australia, where there was no landing tax levied on the ships that carried them. However, they still had to get to the gold mines, which meant they were in for a long and dangerous overland walk.[21]

Hostile miners frequently harassed the Chinese who managed to reach the Australian goldfields. Tensions between European and Australian miners and the Chinese often ran high. Resentment toward the Chinese boiled over in June 1861 when one of the most violent anti-Chinese riots in Australian history erupted: the Lambing Flat riots.

The riot broke out after a bill to restrict Chinese miners failed to pass. Fueled by anger and jealousy, thousands of White miners descended on a Chinese mining camp and attacked its residents. Many Chinese miners were violently beaten, their camps burned, and their belongings destroyed. Some were even scalped by the rioters, while others fled into the nearby bush.

Authorities eventually stepped in, sending police and military forces to restore order. Though some of the main agitators were arrested, none were executed, and many escaped serious punishment altogether. Despite the violence, some Chinese miners returned to the goldfields, determined to continue their work.

One of the more interesting and consequential developments of the gold rush was the decision to phase out the previous convict system of

---

[21] Blainey, Geoffrey. *A Shorter History of Australia.* 1994. Pg. 71.

immigration. Such a change had been in the works for a while. Back in Britain, the notion that convicted criminals were being sent to lands filled with gold, which could lead those convicts to either eventually strike it rich or rob someone else of their riches, began to seem a bit ridiculous to the powers that be. It was determined that the time was ripe to begin the process of phasing out the old system of convict settlers. In December 1852, the British government officially ended all transportation of convicts to the Australian east coast.

By this time, the convicts had already made quite an impact on the culture of Australia. In fact, the legacy of escaped convicts gave rise to the infamous bushrangers. The term was originally used to refer to escaped convicts who hid in the wilderness of the Australian Outback. These escapees often used armed robberies as a means to sustain themselves as they roamed around the range. The term bushranger stuck, and later on, almost any habitual armed robbing gang was referred to as bushrangers. The Ned Kelly gang was among the most infamous (we will talk about him more in the next chapter).

This decade of the gold rush saw the passage of the landmark Australian Colonies Government Act in 1850. This act granted Van Diemen's Land (better known as Tasmania), South Australia, and the colony of Victoria their own legislative councils and allowed for a limited form of representative government.

Because of the gold rush, the emancipation of convicts, and this newfound representation, the Australian colonies experienced a veritable population boom. It is believed that during this period, the population of Australia rose from around 430,000 in 1851 to over one million by 1861. Victoria became the biggest and most heavily populated colony, and Melbourne became the biggest city. Interestingly, Melbourne was also a leader in printed news media, with *The Age* coming to prominence as a popular periodical printed on Australia's newly minted steam-powered printing press. This paper kept Australians up on all of the latest happenings, both near and far. By 1890, it is said to have been regularly selling over 100,000 editions a day, cementing its place as one of the leading papers of the day.

So, the gold rush ultimately led to a population boom and an information explosion. The newly christened railroads and trains helped to carry this information. These stretches of railroad would come to cover much of Australia, and they first began in the city of Melbourne.

The landing at Melbourne in 1840.[10]

All of these things helped to create the perfect backdrop for the noteworthy events to come.

Chapter 5: The Push Inland, Federation, and the Birth of Australia

"The night too quickly passes. And we are growing old. So let us fill our glasses. And toast the Days of Gold. When finds of wondrous treasure, set all the south ablaze. And you and I were faithful mates. All through the roaring days."

-*Henry Lawson*[22]

 From November 1859 to January 1860, a special committee belonging to the Philosophical Institute of Victoria (which would later be renamed the Royal Society) looked into the possibility of exploring the mostly unexplored interior of the Australian Outback. Up until that point, Australia's settlements had mostly been coastal ones. These bold and inquisitive explorers of the committee viewed it as their responsibility—and the responsibility of Queen Victoria's Britain—to push forward into the unknown. Yes, almost like the opening monologue of *Star Trek*, these Australian settlers felt it was their duty to boldly go where no Brit had gone before.

 Queen Victoria's namesake colony, the bustling Australian outpost of Victoria, would lead the charge. Victoria was the richest of the Australian

---

[22] Macintyre, Stuart. A Concise History of Australia. 1999. Pg. 90.

colonies, and it was believed that it was in a prime position to move farther into the Australian interior. This push galvanized the younger generation of Australians. They saw the push into the interior as a push forward for society and civilization in general.

The committee was chaired by Sir William Stawell, who was the Chief Justice of Victoria Supreme Court. The committee members were considered to be refined gentlemen in the traditional British sense of the term. This meant that the leaders of the expedition into the Australian interior were basically from the noble classes of the Anglo-Australian strata, while their subordinates were made up of the lower classes. Those who worked under the leaders of these expeditions ranged from the poor to former convicts to perhaps even a small number of Aboriginals. The latter would have served largely as guides and translators.

Among the leaders of the group were also scientists, such as the esteemed John Macadam, who was a chemist by trade, and Ferdinand von Mueller, who held a PhD in botany. Von Mueller was renowned for his ability to identify and categorize unique flora and fauna in Australia.

Those who headed this expedition placed great trust in recent advances in both communication and transportation. These innovations aided their progress as they pushed farther inland, venturing into harsh and uncharted territories. One notable advancement was the expansion of the overland telegraph, which laid the foundation for faster and more reliable communication between remote regions. The introduction of camel transport, first brought to Australia in the 1860s, also proved invaluable for crossing the arid interior, allowing explorers to carry more supplies over longer distances.

There was also a religious motivation. As Australian historian and writer Manning Clark put it, many Australians felt as if they were somehow being singled out by God to bring about what they viewed as the Christian (at least the Westernized variation) way of life. Surveyor John McDouall Stuart was one of those who firmly believed in this supposed mission. John first attempted an expedition to the Australian interior in November 1859. This mission was largely a bust, and he and his team quickly retreated back to the colonial settlements.

Not to be deterred, Stuart and company made another attempt in March 1860. This time around, they were much more successful and managed to reach the mid-point of the Australian Outback. Here, he and his team raised the British flag. The Union Jack was stuck in a large mound of land that would later be dubbed Central Mount Stuart. The team then traveled another 150 miles northwest before sickness and hunger forced them to turn back.

Another expedition would be launched that fall with the purpose of traveling all the way across the Australian continent. This expedition led by explorers, Robert O'Hara Burke and William John Willis, successfully crossed in a south-north direction, from Melbourne to the Gulf of Carpentaria. Burke and company learned some things along the way from the locals they encountered, including the consumption of a desert plant called nardoo. They had witnessed the locals preparing the stuff and were intrigued. It seemed good enough to them, so the hungry explorers decided to add it to their diet.

Unfortunately for them, they failed to properly roast the plant before grinding it down for consumption, leading to some rather dire results. The nardoo plant has a thiamine (vitamin B1) blocker, which can lead to starvation. The men were puzzled to find that no matter how much nardoo or any other foodstuff they consumed, they were getting skinnier and skinnier. Their bodies were actually being overloaded by thiamine blockers, so they were no longer able to absorb nutrients. Burke and Willis both perished as a result.

This expedition would be followed by another in 1862. It was led by John McDouall Stuart, who helped to map out a large section of the Australian interior. This proved to be crucial for the placing of a telegraph line (the Australian Overland Telegraph Line), which would travel hundreds of miles across Australia. Another milestone was achieved by explorer Ernest Giles, who blazed a path from Adelaide to Perth in 1875.

While Australian explorers were making great inroads across the interior of Australia, the so-called "bushrangers" began to cause trouble in the more established regions. The trouble with the bushrangers had already been brewing before the 1860s, but it escalated following the introduction of the Selection Acts. These acts aimed to break up large squatter-owned landholdings and open up Crown land for purchase by small farmers.

An image of bushrangers.[11]

Two of the most significant acts were the 1861 Crown Lands Alienation Act and the 1861 Crown Lands Occupation Act in New South Wales. Under these laws, settlers—known as "selectors"—could purchase between 40 and 640 acres at one pound per acre, with 20 percent due upfront and the remainder payable over three years.

Other Australian colonies followed suit. Victoria introduced the Duffy Act in 1862, Queensland passed its own Selection Act in 1868, and South Australia followed with the Strangways Act in 1869. These laws encouraged small-scale farming, but they also led to bitter conflicts between selectors and wealthy squatters, who often tried to drive them off the land.

When land prospectors began to utilize loopholes in the ruling to purchase and create monopolies on land holdings, the poor classes began to suffer. They were not only in debt, but they also found themselves the owners of rather unproductive tracts of land in inhospitable environments. The children of these poor farmers often grew up to become desperadoes. The disparities led to resentment, and soon, the perceived freedom of "the bush" came calling. Poor bands of robbers sought to play Robin Hood by imitating the ex-convict bushrangers of the past. The bushranger gangs roamed the wild bushlands, living on the plunder they accumulated. The most famous of these bushranger gangs to rise to prominence was the Ned Kelly gang. Although Ned has become a popular anti-hero of sorts, historian Manning Clark did not pull any punches in his description of him. In his blunt assessment, he stated, "Ned Kelly was a wild ass of a man, snarling, roaring and frothing like a ferocious beast when the tamer entered the cage."[23]

Considering all of the damage he caused, such snap judgments are easy to make. But to be fair, if one simply looked into Ned Kelly's upbringing, it becomes much easier to understand how he ended up the way he did. Ned's dad was sent to Australia from Ireland in 1843 as part of his punishment for stealing a couple of pigs. Shortly after his arrival, he met Ned's mother, Ellen Quinn, who gave birth to Ned in June 1855.

Seemingly doomed from day one, Ned was born with the stigma of being the child of a convict. Ned was raised to distrust authority figures, with his father repeatedly complaining about how those of an Irish background, such as himself, could never expect to get a fair trial at the hands of British authorities.

Ned Kelly's father died in 1866, and his father's passing led that cumbersome chip on Ned's shoulder to only get bigger. His widowed mother took him and his siblings to live on a small plot of land situated at a place called Eleven Mile Creek, which was located somewhere in the middle of the settlements of Glenrowan and Greta.

This section of Australia was a real no man's land back in those days, and many rough and rugged bushrangers passed through. These men greatly influenced Ned, and soon, he was picking up their habits. He became a skilled horse thief early on, learning the art of ambushing unwary travelers.

However, his activities soon got the attention of the police. In 1870, he was arrested by Constable Thomas Lonigan. It is said that Lonigan was pretty rough with Ned and actually dragged him across the ground in the process of taking him into custody.

Several years later, in 1878, matters truly came to a head. On April 15th, 1878, an incident occurred that changed the trajectory of the lives of Ned's whole family. It was on that day that the police arrived at the Kelly homestead with a warrant to arrest one of Ned's brothers for stealing a horse. Constable Fitzpatrick fully expected to take the young man into custody with little to no issue. However, the arresting officer was met by the angry Kelly mother swinging a shovel. Someone from the house fired off a shot, which managed to hit Fitzpatrick in his wrist. The officer was

---

[23] Clark, Manning. *A History of Australia*. 1988.

probably lucky that the Kelly gang did not finish him off then and there. They obviously could have fired a finishing shot, and Ned's mother was right there with a shovel to bury the evidence.

Although they let the officer leave, Ned Kelly warned him not to speak a word of the incident to a soul. Ned must have greatly overestimated his powers of intimidation. If he expected a police officer with a bullet lodged in his wrist to simply forget all about his warrant and tell the folks down at the police station that everything was just fine, he had gravely misunderstood the situation.

The officer reported everything that had occurred, and an arrest warrant was put out for his mother, the shovel-wielding Ellen Kelly. She was taken into police custody while Ned fled to the safety of the bush. From his refuge, he would strike back at the police in a most devastating manner.

Ned Kelly came upon an encampment of police officers on October 26th, 1878, and shot and killed three of them. A fourth man—Constable McIntyre—managed to get away. McIntyre told the rest of the police department about what had happened.

The police were outraged. To see their own officers gunned down was bad enough, but the fact that this gang of bushrangers seemed determined to continually flout the law and live by their own rules was deemed intolerable as it pertained to civil society. Ned and his gang were not just criminals at this point; they were insurrectionist revolutionaries who defied all rules and were attempting to set up their own form of government.

As was the case with Ned Kelly, these bushranger gangs were in constant battles with the police. According to historian Manning Clark, during this period, at least eleven policemen were murdered, and many more were wounded just trying to bring some of these criminals to justice.

Ned Kelly the day before his execution.[12]

Yes, despite some of the later romanticism attached to bushrangers like Ned Kelly, it must be remembered that they were criminals and that their actions led to death and destruction.

Furthermore, the society that so many had been trying to establish in Australia would not survive if such lawlessness was left unchecked. The Australian colonial powers had to either confront and put an end to the bushrangers; if they did not, Australia could devolve into a seething cesspool of chaos and corruption.

Many bushrangers seemed to prefer chaos over an orderly society any day of the week. One infamous bushranger, Ben Hall, terrorized Australia from 1863 to 1865. He went on a rampage of robbing, killing, and destruction that brought Australian civil society to its knees. He was the son of former Australian convicts and seemed to live up to the hellion stereotype of the later bushrangers. As historian Manning Clark described him, "Hall had a private hell in his heart against society in general and the police in particular."[24]

Bushrangers like Hall despised authority and especially hated the police, as was evidenced by the frequent shootouts they had with the cops during the course of their many exploits. Ben Hall was left dead after coming out on the losing end of one of these exchanges. His corpse was found riddled with bullets in May 1865. He was only twenty-seven years old when he was killed.

Ned Kelly met a similar—if perhaps more infamous—fate. Prior to his final showdown, Ned Kelly had been planning one of his boldest and deadliest robberies yet. His plan? To derail and ambush a police train near Glenrowan, Victoria. In preparing for the attack, he and his gang took over the town, holding dozens of locals hostage at the Glenrowan Inn.

As fate would have it, one of those who managed to escape—local schoolteacher Thomas Curnow—would become Kelly's undoing. Curnow convinced the gang to let him leave, claiming he needed to care for his ill wife and child. Ned might have thought he was showing some measure of kindness, but if so, it was the last kind act he would make.

Once freed, Curnow placed a lantern on the railway tracks and frantically signaled the oncoming police train, warning them of the trap

---

[24] Clark, Manning. *A History of Australia*. 1988.

ahead. Instead of blindsiding an unprepared police force, the Kelly gang was the ones being ambushed.

Heavily armed police swarmed the Glenrowan Inn, and an all-night siege began. The building was riddled with bullets; over fifteen thousand rounds were fired. By morning, Ned Kelly, clad in his makeshift armor, emerged from the smoke and gunfire for one final stand. But the police brought him down with shots to his unprotected legs, ending the reign of Australia's most infamous bushranger.[25]

The police leaped upon the armored figure writhing on the ground in agony. Ned reportedly accepted defeat and was placed under police custody without any further incident. His subsequent trial became something of a sensation in Australia, and many still tended to view him sympathetically despite his crimes. Nevertheless, he was found guilty, and on November 11th, 1880, he was executed.

In many ways, as Australian "civilized" society moved farther into the Australian interior, it was those at the margins of society—the bushrangers—who stood up as the last real, formidable impediment of this forward motion of civilization. Many also began to realize that the Selection Acts, which had monopolized land holdings, contributed to the problem of landless rogues turning to a life of crime. This was noted in a local Australian paper called the *Empire* in an article first printed on February 11th, 1867. The article stated, "The end of the present system of land monopoly will involve the end of bushranging. Whenever the interior wilderness is thrown fully open to the industrious cultivator of the soil— when families are allowed to make permanent homes—then and not till then will the bushranging brood be extirpated."[26] Soon enough, it was clear to most Australians that in order to bring about a much-needed change of heart among the lower classes, there would need to be a change in the system of government itself.

In March of 1891, tidings from Queensland, a settlement on the northeastern coast of Australia, were beginning to concern the Australian powers that be. In this part of colonial Australia, disaffected laborers were going on strike, and in one incident, they even burned down several woolsheds in Lorne and Mangroo. Woolsheds were where traditional wool shearers cut wool from sheep.

---

[25] West, Barbara A. *A Brief History of Australia*. 2010. Pg. 70.

[26] Clark, Manning. *A History of Australia*. 1988. Pg. 311.

Those responsible for shearing all of those sheep were not happy with labor conditions. There were the typical complaints of long hours and low pay, but these laborers were also upset with new methodologies that had been introduced. In particular, they took umbrage at the introduction of new fencing that included barbed wire and made the old-fashioned method of sheep shepherding obsolete. They were also frustrated with new machines that were being introduced that threatened to make the job of shearing sheep by hand not even necessary.

At this time, the demand for wool had increased considerably, and the profits of the companies behind this enterprise were increasing. Yet, the people who sheared these sheep felt they were being denied their benefits and even being phased out altogether.

These sheep shearers were indeed upset, and they wanted everyone to know about it. The shearers even went as far as to set the surrounding grasslands ablaze.

At this point, the line between passionate political protest and outright rebellion seemed blurred. Fearing an escalation, Queensland authorities sent in armed police and military forces to restore order. Yet, the wet season's torrential rains turned the roads into muddy, impassable terrain, making it nearly impossible for the authorities to track down the striking shearers.

This emboldened the strikers, who refused to back down. Their demands grew beyond wages and working conditions, with some pushing for greater political representation for workers. However, their fight was soon cut short. In March 1891, police arrested strike leaders, charging them with sedition and conspiracy. The strike was effectively crushed.

While the strike failed, the battle for workers' rights continued at the ballot box. That same year, the Australian Labor Party (ALP) was formed, marking the first time a political party was founded with the working class at its core. Across the colonies, Labor candidates began winning seats. Among them was Adolphus George Taylor, a firebrand politician known for his populist speeches and advocacy for workers' rights. Though not a direct leader of the Labor movement, his rhetoric captured the frustrations of the working class at a time of great change in Australia's political landscape.

Initially, representatives like Taylor focused solely on uniting the working class, but these efforts eventually morphed into uniting the colonies of Australia. The idea of creating a federation of Australian states was viewed as simply the most logical way to unite the native-born European and largely working-class Australians. Unification was viewed as a means of leveraging more power over the often British-born landed elites and company owners, who lorded over the rest of the Australian populace.

By 1890, the idea of a federation was gaining serious momentum. The six colonies—Western Australia, South Australia, Tasmania, Victoria, New South Wales, and Queensland—seemed ripe for unification.

This push for a federation had its early roots in the Federal Council of Australasia, which was formed in 1885 as a representative body for the Australian colonies. However, the council had limited powers, and New South Wales refused to join, believing a stronger national government was needed.

In 1890, colonial representatives met in Melbourne to formally discuss the prospect of a federation. While no immediate decisions were made, the conference paved the way for the 1891 Constitutional Convention in Sydney.

Sir Henry Parkes delivering the first resolution at the federation conference in Melbourne in March 1890.[18]

At this 1891 convention, delegates—including key figures such as Sir Samuel Griffith, Edmund Barton, and Henry Parkes—drafted the first version of the Australian Constitution. However, political divisions and a lack of public support at the time meant the effort stalled. It would take nearly a decade of debating and campaigning before a federation finally became a reality in 1901.

In 1893, another constitutional convention was held. The convention met in the city of Corowa and discussed steps to have elected delegates participate in a referendum across the colonies to endorse a federal constitution. This became known as the Corowa Plan.

More conventions were held in 1897 and 1898, which moved things along even further. A plan had been put forward to establish a constitutional commonwealth of federated Australian states that would still (at least ostensibly) be under the British Crown. In March 1900, delegates were sent to London to get an official federation bill passed. This bill was finally passed on July 5th, 1900, and approved on July 9th. This led to the official declaration of the Commonwealth of Australia on January 1st, 1901.

Chapter 6: World War I and Australia's Increasing Role in Global Conflicts

"Our wounded are most amazing. They sing, they cheer, they smoke their cigarettes."

-*General Sir John Monash*[27]

Just prior to the outbreak of the First World War, the British Empire was at its height, and the average Australian was receiving all of the benefits of its imperial largesse. Even though Australia had become a federation, it was still linked at the hip with Britain. British ideas, goods, and migrants continued to flow freely into Australia. Even as late as 1914, many government positions in Australia were still being taken up by people who had been born in Britain. In 1914, the Australian governor-general was British-born.

Considering as much, when the First World War erupted that very year, it was no surprise that Australia was ready to rally the troops for what was ostensibly a British cause in the fight over hegemony in Europe. This was not the first time that assistance from Australia was expected. During the Second Boer War (1899-1902), Australia delivered military support when British interests in South Africa were threatened.

---

[27] Blainey, Geoffrey. *A Shorter History of Australia*. 1994. Pg. 158.

In order to explain how the Australians became involved in the Boer War, some background is necessary. The Portuguese were the first to make landfall on South Africa's Cape of Good Hope when they circumnavigated the tip of Africa in the late 15th century. The Portuguese originally called it the Cape of Storms due to the turbulent weather conditions often found there. The name was quickly changed to Cabo da Boa Esperança, which translates to "Cape of Good Hope." This name change came about due to the renewed sense of optimism and hope that the circumnavigation of Africa had brought. The Portuguese had now found an alternative route to India and had access to the lucrative Asian trade.

The Portuguese might have been the first Europeans to touch down in the region, but their competitors, the Dutch, were the first to stay. They created a permanent settlement that developed into Cape Town, which then grew into the larger South African settlement of Cape Colony.

The status of the Dutch in the region remained unchanged until the French Revolution brought French troops to the Dutch settlement in 1795. The British, who were battling the French for dominance, arrived right on their heels and seized Cape Colony for themselves. Several years later, the Dutch ended up officially handing the colony over to the British by way of the Anglo-Dutch Treaty of 1814.

But even though the Dutch ceded their territory to the British, many Dutch settlers known as Boers remained. They pushed into frontier country to forge independent settlements during an exodus known as the Great Trek. This resulted in the Dutch-Boer colonies like the Transvaal and the Orange Free State.

However, after some rather lucrative mineral deposits of diamonds and gold were discovered in these regions, the British and Boers began to bump heads, leading to the Boer Wars. With the eruption of the Second Boer War in 1899, many Australian troops were sent to the region to participate in the fighting against the Dutch Boers.

The Australian cavalry units known as lancers played the most pivotal role. These Aussie lancers stormed right into the siege of Kimberley in February 1900. Kimberley was a diamond mining town that had been captured by the Boers, and the Australian lancers helped to break this siege. The Australian troops also played a prominent role in the battles of Paardeberg and Modder River.

The Boers surrendered in May 1902. Britain absorbed the colonies, and in 1910, the region became a self-governing dominion under the British flag. This was all accomplished with the help of their Australian allies.

Back in the days of the Boer Wars, it seemed that British and Australian cooperation was expected. However, as it pertains to World War I, many modern-day historians have expressed surprise at how eager the Australians were to provide military assistance. Part of this eagerness was due to the closely perceived historical and cultural ties between Australia and Britain.

However, there was a more pragmatic reason to support the British as well. The Australians viewed the British as their protectors. The British navy and its ability to project power far and wide kept many possible threats at bay.

Japan had risen up as a world power by this point, and there was great fear that the Japanese might one day threaten Australia. The events of World War II would prove that these fears were not unfounded. There were also other actors in the region that could have turned hostile to Australian interests if the British were not there to enforce the status quo.

The Australians, therefore, very much believed that the defense of Britain was in their own best interest. During World War I, the principal foe—Germany—made inroads in Australia's backyard. The Germans had a colonial outpost in what we now call Papua New Guinea.

The large island just north of Australia is referred to as New Guinea as a whole, and it has a rather complicated history. Just prior to World War I, the island was split up between the French, British, and Germans. The French controlled the western half of the island, the British controlled the southeastern portion, and the Germans controlled the northeastern portion.

After the outbreak of World War I, the German outpost in the northeast of the island became a front line of the war. In the early stages of the conflict, Australian naval units seized Rabaul, a strategic port in German New Guinea. The Australian armed forces also seized the German island of Nauru, seizing control of a German radio station in the process.

Another early incident involved an Australian naval vessel opening fire on a German warcraft called the *Emden*. The German ship was pulverized and made inoperable.

Australia's naval forces proved themselves battle-ready in these early exchanges. This was an important test since Australia's navy was relatively new. It was only in 1909 that Australia's dominion fleet was approved.

After these early naval exchanges in and around Australian territory, the Australian armed forces began to be transferred to take up the fight in Europe and the Middle East. One of Germany's main allies in the war was the Ottoman Empire, whose heart lay in Istanbul (previously Constantinople), Turkey. The British were eager to open up a front here. The goal was to knock the Turks out of the war and open up a supply line over the Black Sea to nearby Russia, which was fighting on the side of the Allies.

The Russians were already faltering at this point due to domestic problems, and they were in dire need of supplies. The Russians had a massive army but were often seriously lacking in equipment. There were even instances in which threadbare Russian troops faced off against their foes barefoot. Britain and France hoped to provide proper equipment to their Russian ally, lest the Germans, who were tearing through the Eastern Front, brought the Russians to their knees.

This was all part of the Gallipoli campaign. This campaign was named after the narrow strip of land that reaches across the Dardanelles to the Turkish mainland, where British and Australian troops had landed. The British war planners seemed to think that marching along this narrow peninsula would be easy, but it was not. In fact, it was a horrendous nightmare. The troops were squeezed into very narrow, close quarters and had to battle their way through intense and determined machine gun fire.

During this struggle, the Australians were part of a special group of fighters that included troops from neighboring New Zealand. The contingent was dubbed the Australian and New Zealand Army Corps, or "ANZAC" for short. It is said that around eight thousand Australians were killed in this melee.

After about eight months, the British high command was mortified to have to order a withdrawal. It was deemed too hard and too costly to continue the mission. The last Australian troops evacuated this death trap just a few days before Christmas in 1915.

Nevertheless, many Australians viewed this unmitigated disaster as a baptism of fire that brought them onto the world stage as serious participants in international affairs. Even though the mission was a failure, the brave Australians who were willing to sacrifice their lives would be forever remembered on ANZAC Day. This is an officially designated national holiday in Australia that is celebrated on April 25th. Although the holiday began in remembrance of those who fought and died during this doomed military operation in World War I, it later became a memorial day that celebrated those who had served or died in wars.

After the failed Gallipoli campaign, many Australians began to be sent in large numbers to France, the Western Front of the war. They soon found themselves fighting trench warfare, which was just about as brutal and static as what they had faced in Turkey. Soldiers from all of the Allied countries were dying at an appalling rate.

It was soon decided that a rapid recruitment drive was needed. There just were not enough soldiers to fight on the Western Front. Australia was tapped to send even more soldiers. This led W. M. Hughes, the Labor prime minister, to start a draft of army-age men so that they could be sent to France. The decision became an unpopular one as the war continued, and in November 1916, the Labor Party faced consequences at the ballot box.

Voters were upset because of the draft and the economic toll that the war was taking on life back home in Australia. Both the cost of food and the price of rent had gone up considerably, significantly affecting working-class Australians. By 1917, most Australians were feeling the bite of inflation. Meanwhile, the political elites continued to try to sell their war aims.

Australians in Egypt in 1914. The kangaroo was their mascot.[14]

Nevertheless, the war dragged on, and in 1917, Australian troops took part in the epic Battle of Gaza. The Levant, a region home to modern-day nation-states and territories such as Israel and Palestine, was still under the dominion of the Ottoman Empire at that time. The British and their Australian allies duked it out with the Turks here as well.

As successful as the Turks were at defending the Turkish homeland, they could not defend this territory too terribly well. The British and their allies won the day here, and the whole region became a British mandate. Eventually, it would be carved up into the nations and territories we have come to recognize today. Of course, the history of the Middle East is much more complicated than that simple summary, and ownership of these lands has changed many times over the past few thousand years or so.

World War I would come to a close on November 11th, 1918, when the defeated Germans signed an armistice. Australian troops did not participate in the Allied occupation of Germany since Australian Prime Minister Hughes felt it was in the nation's best interest to return their fighting men back to Australia as soon as possible.

Upon their return, they were met by many Australians who had some rather ambivalent feelings about the war. Additionally, many of these troops were not exactly in a celebratory mood. Why did they fight? Just to support Britain? Although the fight was argued to be in Australia's best interest, many in the public failed to see it.

Even worse, the war had been a costly one for Australia. There were even difficulties coming up with the finances to dole out the pensions expected from all of the returning soldiers, many of whom had been rendered permanently disabled. Others faced chronic nervous conditions, which back then would have been referred to as shell shock. This disorder was called as such because it was felt that the shock of hearing the blasting of artillery shells and other loud explosions over a long, sustained period created an acute nervous condition in soldiers. Now, we are more likely to refer to such a distressed state as being PTSD or post-traumatic stress disorder.

To treat these distressed veterans, the Returned Services League, or RSL, was put in place. First established in 1916 while the war was still raging, the RSL spearheaded special programs and facilities to aid veterans who had just returned from the front.

Australian politicians often spoke of crafting legislation that would make Australia a land fit for heroes. In many ways, though, this idyllic postwar vision failed to come to fruition. Most glaring is the fact that Aboriginal veterans were not even eligible to participate in any of the programs designed for veterans of the First World War. They were denied any further medical care and not allowed to take part in a special soldier resettlement program that gave returning Australian servicemen of European ancestry land to settle. This was indeed unsettling since many Indigenous Australians had agreed to take up Australia's fight in order to gain more rights for their people. Instead, they returned home to face more of the same poor treatment.

Nevertheless, for many who had traveled far and wide fighting under the banner of Australia, a fire had been lit within them. During the interwar period between World War I and World War II, the quest for equal rights and a more inclusive Australian society began to take shape.

Chapter 7: The Interwar Period, Aboriginal Rights, and a Stolen Generation

It is estimated that out of the 324,000 some Australians who took part in the war to end all wars (World War I), around 60,000 were killed, and around 150,000 suffered significant injuries. Despite this high toll, the war had some positive outcomes for Australia. The war brought more mobility for the average working-class Australian. It became easier for them to attain high positions in the military and government administration, positions that were not normally open to them.

Even so, these Australians were outliers. Unemployment became a real problem in the immediate postwar period. By 1921, unemployment had risen to as much as 13 percent. Australia was also lagging behind the times compared to much of the rest of the industrialized world as it pertained to items of modern convenience.

In the early 1920s, Britain and the United States were enjoying automobiles, radios, telephones, and the like. Meanwhile, Australians were not quite so privileged. By and large, Australians were still cooking with wood stoves, and firewood was the primary means of keeping warm. Food was more likely to be stored underground in cellars, and the modern convenience of the refrigerator was still largely unknown.

The same could be said for the new-fangled washers and dryers. Australians were still washing and drying their garments by hand. In fact,

Monday was widely known as "washing day" all across Australia. This was the day that clothes could be seen hanging from clotheslines in just about every Australian yard.

Most Australian homes also lacked phones. The phone was seen as more of a fixture for an upscale office than an actual mainstay for the home. The reason behind this perceived backwardness was due to a combination of factors. For one thing, Australia was, in many ways, still considered a far-flung, remote outpost. This was before the days of regular passenger airliners. Travel to Australia was largely relegated to boats, which had to spend months traveling across the high seas. As such, it was much harder for Australia to stay on top of the latest innovations and trends.

However, as much as these descendants of Australia's European colonizers might have lagged behind their industrialized peers, this perceived gap was nothing compared to what the Aboriginal descendants faced. Having lived long on the fringes of Australian colonial society, the Aboriginals had been pushed to the side. Many were grouped together on so-called "mission settlements," which historian Stuart Macintyre described as a process that made them veritable wards of the state.

Even worse was the practice of taking Aboriginal children away from their parents in order to educate them in the ways of "civilized" society. It was believed that the new generations of Aboriginals could be taught to forget about their past and trained for integration into the larger society. It was believed that as these new generations were integrated with the rest of Australia, the mission settlements that looked after the Aboriginals could be dismantled and shut down.

This generation of children, who had been snatched from their parents to be trained in Western ways of thinking, would make up what has been termed the "stolen generation." Many Aboriginal descendants look back on these past actions in horror and describe such things as nothing short of cultural genocide.

During this period, Australian society was not the most receptive to such movements. Australia, just like much of the rest of the world, was rocked by the Great Depression. The Great Depression had started thousands of miles away in the United States when the stock market crashed. Even the most enlightened Australian would have been hard-pressed not to put such lofty notions (at least lofty considering the time period) like Aboriginal rights on the back burner when their own families faced dire deprivation.

Demonstrating just how much the fortunes of countries had become intertwined with each other, this downturn in the United States had ripple effects all across the planet. Times soon became hard in Australia, and by the mid-1930s, the unemployment rate had climbed as high as 21 percent.

Nevertheless, the nascent Aboriginal rights groups began to clamor for more rights. The economic downturn only served as further impetus to take a stand against what had been a long-standing and egregious oppression. They demanded an end to the practice of taking children away from their families and for more inclusion into Australian society.

During this difficult era, Aboriginal groups formed what was eventually called the Aborigines Progressive Association. This group gained widespread attention on January 26th, 1938, for staging the Day of Mourning to commemorate Arthur Phillip's landfall on Australian shores, which kickstarted the forcible displacement of their people. These progressive Aboriginals also called for policy changes that would grant them full citizenship and equality under the Australian government.

The Aboriginals seemed to have reached a sober conclusion. They concluded that they had been done a terrible wrong, but since there was no changing the past, and since the overthrow of the current regime was unlikely, they should at the very least be accorded the same constitutional rights that the descendants of their colonial oppressors enjoyed.

The group did gain the ear of the Australian government, and meetings were even held with the prime minister. The prime minister took their calls for more rights seriously and convened a panel of experts to try to find a better path forward. This panel of experts included everyone from administrators to psychologists to even anthropologists.

Anthropologists suggested that Aboriginal culture should not be suppressed. According to historian Stuart Macintyre, one of these anthropologists, A. P. Elkin, who was a professor of anthropology at the University of Sydney at the time, suggested that Australian administrators should not suppress Aboriginal culture but instead use it as a tool to better the Aboriginals. As Elkin put it, the efforts should be designed to "help them to develop further along their own cultural lines."[28]

These suggestions by Elkin led to calls for an Aboriginal administration that would be informed by anthropological expertise. This new approach

---

[28] Macintyre, Stuart. A Concise History of Australia. 1999.

was dubbed the "New Deal for Aborigines." The stated aim of this effort was to uplift the Aboriginals and extend to them the ordinary rights of citizenship.

In an article from the popular Melbourne newspaper *The Argus*, dated December 14th, 1938, the basic tenets of this supposed "New Deal" were laid out. Some of the terminology and expressions used are a bit shocking to modern sensibilities since they blatantly categorized Indigenous peoples based on the amount of Indigenous ancestry that flows through their veins. It even makes mention of those who are perceived to be "fully detribalized."

Considering that this was happening during the time of the popular Great Depression-era programs called the New Deal in the United States, spearheaded by Democrat President Franklin Delano Roosevelt, the name is likely not a coincidence. The title seems to suggest great and transformative changes. However, there was nothing really all that progressive about this program as it pertained to the expansion of Aboriginal rights.

On the contrary, it amounted to what Stuart Macintyre described as "extending the practice of forcible removal of Aboriginal children from their families."[29] The provisions merely sought to categorize those who were considered "detribalized" enough to be snatched up and forcibly "educated" about what was deemed to be proper Australian society.

At this point in Australian history, it seemed that there was a two-pronged approach to the integration of Aboriginal descendants into Australian society. On the one hand, you had a panel of anthropologists headed by Elkin stating that Aboriginal culture should be embraced rather than oppressed, and on the other, you had administrators such as A. O. Neville, who held the rather dubious distinction of being the chief protector of Aboriginals in Western Australia, who insisted that the practice of child removal with the intent of instilling Western values in them was the way forward.

As much as this debate raged and despite all of the terrible consequences that were brought about, all talk of this matter would get shelved with the outbreak of World War II. The outbreak of the war created an existential threat that seemed to temporarily make these matters moot—the potential invasion of Japan.

---

[29] Macintyre, Stuart. A Concise History of Australia. 1999.

Chapter 8: Australia during World War II

"Nothing would come to the men and women of the working class as a gift from the gods. Everything they gained had to be fought for."
   -*Australian Prime Minister, John Curtin*[30]

The Australian government and its armed forces were pulled into World War II in very much the same way they had been pulled into World War I. Britain had announced its intention to go to war, and Australia, as the most loyal of its allies, followed suit.

Britain had been unsuccessfully trying to avert war by appeasing fascist dictators. Italy's invasion of Ethiopia in 1935 was largely ignored, as was Japan's aggression in China. German aggression in Europe was not entirely ignored, but every trespass was negotiated away. The British under Prime Minister Neville Chamberlain felt they were keeping the peace by appeasing the Germans when they swallowed up the Rhineland, the Sudetenland, Czechoslovakia, and even Austria.

However, when the Germans invaded Poland in September 1939, it was finally considered a bridge too far, and the British, along with their French allies, declared war. After the war was officially declared, Australian Prime Minister Robert Menzies likewise announced that it was his "duty" to let his Australian countrymen know that they, too, were at war with Germany and its allies.

---

[30] Macintyre, Stuart. A Concise History of Australia. 1999. Pg. 197.

Prime Minister Menzies with Prime Minister Churchill.[15]

Menzies is an iconic character in the history of Australia. He first served as prime minister from 1939 to 1941 before falling out of favor with his political party. Menzies later came back in a big way when he was elected as prime minister again in 1949. He went on to serve until 1966. As of this writing, he is Australia's longest-serving prime minister.

Although Germany was the principal foe in Europe at the outset of World War II, the true menace to Australians was Germany's wartime ally, Japan. Japan had been ramping up its aggression in the region for years and was looking for any excuse to start seizing territory in and around Australia.

The threat to Australia was considerable, but even so, something of a malaise had taken hold of the Australian public when it came to war. Unlike the First World War, which saw young Australian men enthusiastically volunteer as if they were about to set off on the greatest of adventures, the Australians were decidedly less enthused about this latest brewing conflict. It's said that only twenty thousand Australians volunteered in the opening stages of this war, even though Britain was putting pressure on Australia to come up with a formidable fighting force by the fall of 1939.

However, during the interwar period, Australia had lowered its capability to orchestrate a robust military effort. In truth, the Australians had become too dependent on the British Royal Navy. The British, as overstretched as they were, soon became unable to provide a robust protection of Australian interests. By the summer of 1940, France had already been knocked out of the war, and Britain was looking for any help it could find. Initially, the military planners desired to have Australians shipped over to France, just like in World War I, but France's quick capitulation changed those plans. There would be no repeat like the Western Front of World War I in this quick-moving war.

After the fall of France, Italy's dictator, Benito Mussolini, officially threw in his lot with Hitler and declared war on Britain. This meant that Australia was at war with Italy as well. Italy's entry into the war opened up a whole new front since Italy had extensive colonial holdings in North Africa. Many of them, such as Italy's colonial holdings in Libya, butted right up against British colonial territory. British outposts in Egypt and Sudan were now wedged between Italian Libya and Italian-occupied Ethiopia. Threatened on all sides, the British deployed in North Africa desperately needed an influx of reinforcements. The Australians provided this boost to British morale.

Australians and troops from British-controlled India poured into the region in November 1940. The Australians fought hard. In early 1941, they enjoyed a string of victories, such as the Battle of Bardia on January 3rd, the Battle of Tobruk on January 22nd, and the Battle of Benghazi on February 7th. The Australians are said to have suffered some 130 deaths in the Battle of Bardia alone. Nevertheless, this battle was viewed as a stunning success and was a great morale booster since it was able to bring back a sense of forward momentum among the Allied troops, who had been increasingly put on the defensive ever since the fall of France.

The Allies (which at that point consisted mostly of Britain, the freedom fighters of Free France, and dominion troops such as the Australians) were literally on the march. They were battling it out in the Mediterranean Sea.

Australian naval forces took on Italian ships and submarines. The Italian submarines tried their best to keep British and Australian craft at bay but were ultimately outdone. Several Italian submarines were sunk.

With more freedom to move across the shorelines of North Africa, Australian naval craft were able to punish Italian positions on the ground with naval bombardments from the water. This proved a great aid to future ground operations against Italian positions.

Along with taking on the Italians, the Australian forces also attempted to open up a second front in Africa by taking on the forces of Vichy France. Vichy France was the rump state that had formed in southern France around the town of Vichy, France, after France's defeat at the hands of the Germans. This French government was essentially a German puppet state. Although it claimed neutrality, it was a passive ally of Germany; as such, the British and Australians viewed Vichy France as a legitimate target.

The battlecruiser *Australia* made its way to French-controlled Senegal and tried to seize this piece of prized wartime territory from Vichy France. The French fighters positioned there showed that they would not be easily overcome. They put up such a stiff resistance that the plan was aborted, and the Australian battlecruiser retreated.

One of the most notable successes of the Australian fleet in the region occurred on July 19th, 1941. On this day, the Australian battleship *Sydney* managed to sink the Italian battleship *Bartolomeo Colleoni*. This battleship was named after the famed captain general of the Republic of Venice, who had the same name. Bartolomeo Colleoni went down in history as one of the most brilliant Italian tacticians. The fact that his namesake ship was sunk and destroyed likely seemed like a bad omen to the Italians.

The Italians seemed to be fighting a losing battle at this point, and around this time, they were being beaten on an entirely different front. The Italians had shot across the Mediterranean and attempted an ill-prepared invasion of Greece. The invasion was first launched in the fall of 1940, but by the spring of 1941, the Greeks were steadily pushing the Italians out. It seemed as if the Italians were in for a humiliating defeat until the Germans poured in to reinforce Italian positions. Like the movement of chess pieces on a wartime chessboard, this change of dynamics in Greece soon affected the North African theater as well.

The British sought to avoid a complete collapse of Greece and felt compelled to send their own troops to fight off the Germans and Italians in Greece. They also made sure to bring some Australian troops with them. The Australian 6th Division was sent to Greece that April.

However, this repositioning of troops meant that positions in North Africa would become more vulnerable. This increasing vacuum meant greater demands were placed on the Australians to fill in the gaps. Even more young Australian men were sent abroad into these increasingly volatile theaters of war.

In some ways, Australian leadership felt as if the Australian armed forces were being yanked around a bit too much by the British high command. They also did not feel as if they were being appreciated for all of the efforts they were making. The growing feelings of frustration led Australian Prime Minister Robert Menzies to head to London in 1941 to discuss how the war was shaping up. During the course of this discussion, Robert Menzies suggested that British Prime Minister Winston Churchill should give the Australians more independence when it came to British decision-making. He even suggested establishing a special war cabinet of dominion leaders such as himself.

Menzies was disappointed in Churchill's reaction. At times, Churchill was rather dismissive. He seemed to think that the Australian armed forces should be at the beck and call of the British and have no say from their own Australian leadership. Australian leadership had traditionally deferred to the British, but there was an increasing desire to position Australian forces closer to home to defend the Australian mainland.

These feelings sharpened to a razor's edge in December of 1941 when Japan went on the offensive and bombed a US naval base in Hawaii. Several Japanese battalions made landfall in Singapore on February 8th, 1942. Just prior to the Japanese invasion, British forces in the region had been supplemented by an additional two thousand Australian troops on January 24th. The Australian troops were not given a very prominent role in this struggle and were often relegated to backup and fallback positions. The British would later lodge many complaints about the Australian recruits, claiming that they behaved in an unprofessional manner and that there were widespread incidents of drunkenness among them.

Whatever was going on, it seemed that the Australian contingent was not happy being in Singapore and not happy with the roles that the British had given them in this struggle against the Japanese. It was almost as if they were reliving the animosity of their penal colony days when Australian convict settlers stood at odds with distinguished British officers. To put it simply, the Australians and the British rubbed each other the wrong way.

British complaints about their Australian auxiliaries became even more cutting in the last hours of Singapore's defense. There were accusations of Australians abandoning their posts and even attempting to requisition naval craft in order to escape the battle. In the end, Singapore was lost to the British. The British lost an important outpost in the region as a result.

The Japanese could now drive deep, right into Australia's own backyard, with very little to hinder their progress. The overstretched British had already cut their losses. They determined that it was in their best interest to focus most of their effort against Adolf Hitler in Europe and North Africa. So, Japan's aggression was essentially placed on the back burner.

Such a thing might have been in the best interest of Britain, which was attempting to stave off an all-out invasion of the British Isles by German forces, but it certainly was not in the best interest of the Australians. They knew that Japan was their most immediate and dire threat to their own national survival.

Britain and Australia, which had once been firmly joined together, began what could be termed a long and complicated divorce. Instead of turning toward the already overloaded British for support, the Australians turned toward the Americans. The Americans proved better capable of fighting a two-front war. As the US Armed Forces launched an invasion of North Africa to assist the British in taking on German and Italian troops, they also quickly reconstituted their navy and sent a formidable fighting force into the Pacific to try to halt the Japanese advance.

Around this time, a Labor Party candidate named John Curtin rose to the office of prime minister. He lifted the curtain on the growing drift from Britain and looked toward the United States in this existential conflict. Prime Minister Curtin declared, "Without any inhibitions of any kind, I make it quite clear that Australia looks to America, free of any pangs as to our traditional links of kinship with the United Kingdom."[31]

Further cementing this shift away from Britain was the fact that Australia declared war on Japan without consulting Britain. Previously, such a thing would have been unheard of, but considering the dire straits

---

[31] West, Barbara A. *A Brief History of Australia*. 2010. Pg. 34.

that Australia was in, any outside observer could understand why such an action was taken. In light of the Japanese onslaught, Australia was in a fight for its very survival.

This break with London seemed to have been further formalized a short time later with the Statute of Westminster Adoption Act, which was adopted in 1942. The statute had been introduced several years prior and called for a move toward Australian sovereignty. The 1942 statute made such dreams a reality. It was this statute that enabled Australia to have full control over its foreign affairs, including the ability to declare war on foreign nations if necessary (even though in practice Australia had already done so against Japan). With the threat of outside invasion imminent and with Britain seemingly unable to render appropriate aid, Australia made up its mind to handle its own affairs and finally ratified the statute.

The Japanese ramped up their attacks in the region, raiding both Darwin and Sydney. Even worse, they occupied Papua New Guinea, just to Australia's north. As the Americans slowly moved across the Pacific, Australia became an important outpost. It was viewed as a fallback position in the midst of the bloody carnage that was taking place.

US General Douglas MacArthur would take control of military operations in the region in March 1942. By this time, the Japanese had installed themselves in Papua New Guinea, and by September 1942, they were within marching distance of the modern-day capital of Papua New Guinea, Port Moresby. Australian troops, along with local Papuan auxiliaries, engaged in ferocious battles with the Japanese to stop their advance.

One of these fateful battles was the Battle of Kokoda Track, which is said to have killed some twelve thousand Japanese. The Japanese apparently got the worst of it, as only an estimated two thousand Australians perished. This was, of course, a huge loss of life, but the number was nowhere near as staggering as what the Japanese had suffered.

The battles were quite ferocious, and much of the fighting was infused with an intense hatred. The Australians had a special animosity for the Japanese, whom they often likened to "wild beasts." The fact the Japanese were notoriously brutal to any prisoners of war they captured did not do much to diminish this ferocious and beastly image. The Japanese were known to defy conventional wartime standards as it pertained to the treatment of prisoners of war, starving, beating, and making them march for long hours until they dropped dead.

An Australian machine gun team in Wewak, Papua New Guinea.[16]

The fighting against the Japanese in Papua New Guinea was the most significant land campaign for the Australian armed forces during this conflict. After Japan was halted by the United States at the bloody Battle of Midway, ending their advance across the Pacific, the Australians were relegated to a largely auxiliary and even a kind of "mop-up" role. They had to defer to the United States in any matters of importance. When the war came to a close in 1945, Australia was not privy to talks of how the postwar world would shape up.

After it was all said and done, the Australians lost around thirty-seven thousand troops. Many Australians had been taken as prisoners of war. It is said that of the estimated twenty-two thousand Australians to be captured by the Japanese, only a mere fourteen thousand would live to be repatriated back to Australia at the war's conclusion.

These prisoners of war were used as slave labor by the Japanese to build roads, railroad tracks, and other infrastructure. Many of these unfortunate souls were literally worked to death. One can only imagine how cruel of a sight it must have been to see an emaciated Australian prisoner of war being forced at gunpoint to hammer away at a set of railroad tracks, only to suddenly give out and collapse.

Dutch and Australian prisoners of war in Thailand.[17]

Along with the hardships faced by Australian troops, the average Australian also had to endure the hardships of war—albeit in a much milder variation—such as the shortages of supplies, increased prices for food, rent, and services, and the constant fear of invasion.

After the war, Australia took on a greater role on the world stage. With the help of the US and its Lend-Lease Program, they were able to rebuild and, perhaps even more importantly, modernize. The United States ultimately provided more help in this regard than the British had previously supplied and would continue to do so in the decades to come.

Chapter 9: Immigration, Revitalization, and the Shaping of Modern Australia

In the aftermath of World War II, Australians not only had to rebuild the lagging infrastructure of their nation but also had to come to grips with what it actually meant to be Australian. Australians questioned their convict roots, their status as European supplanters, Aboriginal rights, and new waves of immigrants. Who were they? And more importantly, who did they want to be as a nation?

It was around this time that Australian politicians, such as Labor Party leader Arthur Calwell, began speaking of the so-called "New Australians." This was a term used to describe the forces that were shaping modern Australia. Calwell was an advocate for immigration in order to bolster Australia, which he viewed as being significantly underpopulated. However, there was a catch in Calwell's plans for immigration. He advocated—and later implemented as minister for immigration—the White Australia policy.

An anti-immigration cartoon published in 1888.[18]

The White Australia Policy was one of the most defining and controversial policies in Australian history. First introduced in 1901, it was designed to keep Australia "white" by severely restricting non-European immigration. Through harsh laws like the Immigration Restriction Act, the government ensured that Chinese, Pacific Islanders, and other non-White migrants were excluded from the country.

For decades, Australia remained almost exclusively Anglo-European, rejecting even Jewish refugees fleeing Nazi Germany in the 1930s. However, after World War II, pressure began to build. After the war, most immigrants were displaced refugees fleeing war-ravaged regions of Europe. Many of these immigrants from Europe were Jewish survivors of the Holocaust. According to historian Stuart Macintyre's analysis, in the decade following World War II, Australia welcomed about a million immigrants, with a large majority of them coming from Germany, Greece, the Netherlands, and Italy.

Australia also saw an increase in Chinese migration, particularly from refugees fleeing communist China after 1949. However, many faced resistance, as Australia's White Australia Policy was still in effect, restricting non-European immigration.

Australians were clearly trying to reinforce their perceived European heritage with their immigration policy. Nevertheless, Australians were becoming more keenly aware that they were an outpost of European descendants in a largely non-European region. The sudden independence of neighboring Indonesia only seemed to highlight that point.

Prior to World War II, Indonesia was controlled by the Dutch. In fact, it was referred to as the Dutch East Indies. The Japanese made short work of that when they invaded and occupied the Indonesian archipelago. Even after the Japanese were defeated and kicked out, the Dutch were unable to regain control.

The locals were tired of being lorded over by foreigners and were ready to take matters into their own hands. They launched a brief war of independence in 1947 and successfully sent the Dutch packing. Australia now had a neighboring country that was both non-European and non-Christian (Indonesia is a Muslim-majority country).

Religious preferences did not concern Australians during this period. However, Marxist ideologies raised alarm bells. China officially became communist in 1949, and the Cold War between the Marxist ideologies of the communist bloc versus the capitalist and democratic ideals of the Western world (including Australia) was just getting started.

Even though a war had just ended, there were many in Australia and much of the rest of the world who could not help but wonder when the next conflict would begin. The creation of nuclear weapons led to concern that this conflict could be much more devastating. It was for this reason that Australia began to look toward the newly formed United Nations to try to avert a potential calamity of epic proportions.

The Cold War had just erupted, and due to their past experience of being caught by surprise by external aggression, there were many nervous Australian officials who began to look anxiously toward the Soviet Union and China. Although both of these nations were allies during World War II, communist ideology made them potential adversaries in the eyes of capitalist nations.

China was still in the infancy of its communist transformation but was likely more threatening to Australians because of its closer proximity. To this day, China presents a grave threat to Australia. Australia has even partnered with its one-time enemy Japan (along with the United States) as a means to deter communist China.

Nevertheless, immigrants continued to be drawn to Australia, largely because of the stability of its governance and economic opportunities. The new immigrants who arrived on Australian shores found Australia in the midst of a postwar industrial boom. Many people found jobs in manufacturing-based industries or major public works projects. The building of hydroelectric dams and other kinds of power stations used these new immigrants as a source of labor.

Between 1945 and 1985, around four million immigrants relocated to Australia. Many countries around the world actively tried to limit immigration, so Australia's eagerness to increase the number of immigrants was rather unique. Also, by the 1960s, the White Australia Policy was being slowly dismantled. By 1973, the White Australia Policy was officially abolished, and in the years that followed, Australia became one of the most multicultural nations in the world.

Sydney sometime around 1945.[19]

However, these so-called "New Australians" were not always welcomed by the Old Australians. Nevertheless, the labor pool was certainly welcome and arrived at a crucial juncture. Europe was still crawling out of the rubble, wreck, and ruin of the last world war. While their European peers were trying to rebuild, Australia was given a grand opportunity to finally catch up and climb the industrial ladder. Determined to become an industrial hub, Australia was able to build a wide variety of factories to produce all manner of goods that could be exported all over the world.

During the dark and uncertain days of the Cold War, Australia also made the most of its newfound partnership with the United States. In 1951, a formal coalition was created between Australia, New Zealand, and the United States, which was referred to as ANZUS. This was a security pact in which all parties agreed to take action if any one of them were attacked. Many in the Australian public were relieved to have the protection of the United States military in case an external threat ever arose. This pact would remain in force over the next several decades. The United States suspended its obligations to New Zealand in 1986, but as of this writing, it remains in force between Australia and the United States.

With their security seemingly assured, Australians—both of the old and the new variety—entered into a period of prosperity. The Australian economy of the 1950s and 1960s was booming. Fueled by post-war reconstruction, rapid industrialization, and a growing workforce, the nation entered a period of unprecedented prosperity. The economy grew at an average rate of over 4 percent per year, and for much of the 1960s, unemployment sat at a remarkable low of just 1.5 percent to 2.5 percent.

Manufacturing was on the rise, with industries producing everything from automobiles to household appliances. The Holden car, first produced in 1948, became a symbol of Australia's industrial success, and by the 1960s, there was one car for every 3.5 Australians—an astonishing leap from 1 per 14 people in 1946.

Australia's wealth was also tied to its vast natural resources. Exports of wool, wheat, and minerals surged, helping the nation establish strong trade ties with Asia and beyond. By the late 1960s, Australia had transformed into a modern industrial economy, setting the stage for its continued growth in the decades to come.

However, the Cold War conflict in Vietnam forced the Australians to make good on their pact with the United States. As the United States became more involved in the battlefields of Southeast Asia, Australia was expected to contribute to the war effort.

The Australian government first began by sending military advisors. In the late 1960s, Australian troops put their boots on the ground. It is said that by 1967, there were 6,300 Australians fighting in Vietnam. These Australians came from all walks of life and from all backgrounds.

These Australians—just like their American counterparts—soon began to hear all kinds of dreadful news reports of just how bloody and seemingly intractable the Vietnam conflict was. Australian battalions withstood the infamous Tet Offensive in late 1968, which saw both the North Vietnamese troops and their underground auxiliaries, the Viet Cong, join forces to stage a surprise massive assault deep in the heart of South Vietnam. The Australians and their allies stood strong and ultimately beat their opponents back, but it came at a bloody cost. Even worse, much of the carnage on the ground was widely documented and seemed to solidify the notion in the public's mind that Vietnam was an unwinnable war.

After several years of fighting, it seemed that the war was nowhere near the end. No one likes it their nation's youth is killed and maimed in what seems to be an endless and seemingly unwinnable war. Considering as much, protests began to bubble up in Australia. In 1968, the younger generations began to mobilize in the streets to protest Australia's involvement in Vietnam. These protests later crystallized in 1970, as large-scale demonstrations were held in opposition to the war. The younger generation's vocal opposition to the war and a new set of liberal values began to reshape modern Australian society.

The protest against the war led to other social activism, such as Australia's women's liberation movement, which came to prominence in Adelaide in 1969. The 1970s also saw a revitalized movement for Aboriginal rights. Yes, both new and old Australians alike would have a hand in shaping the Australia we know today.

Chapter 10: The Economy and Environmental and Political Challenges

"When my father was alive, this is what he taught me. He had taught me traditional ways like traditional designs in the body or head of kangaroo Dreaming (that's what we call marlu Dreaming) and eagle Dreaming. He taught me how to sing songs for the big ceremonies. People who are related to us in a close family, they have the have the same sort of jukurrpa Dreaming, and to sing songs in the same way as we do our actions like dancing and paintings on our body or shields or things, and this is what my father taught me. My Dreaming is the kangaroo Dreaming, the eagle Dreaming and the budgerigar Dreaming, so I have three kinds of Dreaming in my jukurrpa and I have to hang onto it."

-*Paddy Japaljarri*[32]

In the latter half of the 20th century, Australia faced plenty of challenges. US President Jimmy Carter was struggling to get a grip on rising gas and grocery store prices in the late 1970s. The Australian economy faced strikingly similar issues of inflation.

During this period, the Australian economy was wide open to outside investors, leading to an increase in privatization. Economic matters, in

---

[32] Macintyre, Stuart. A Concise History of Australia. 1999. Pg. 10.

general, had taken on a much more global scope. Australia even became closer partners with many East Asian countries.

Part of the stability that Australia enjoyed during this period can be attributed to the fact that its two main political parties were not all that different. They had some differences, to be sure, but as it pertained to major policies that would affect the Australian way of life, they both tended to go down a middle road. According to writer and historian John H. Chambers, a strong sense of Australian nationalism prevailed amongst the majority of Australians after Gough Whitlam's Labor government in the mid-1970s.

Gough Whitlam was an interesting figure, to say the least. He was often described as a big man with a lot of big ideas. Whitlam imparted upon Australia a heady dose of new legislation aimed at taking the Australian homeland to the world stage.

Whitlam was seen as an ingenious orator with an incredible wit. He always seemed to know exactly the right thing to say at the right moment, and he absolutely dominated Australian politics. As historian Geoffrey Blainey once put it, "he could not ride a wave without commanding it to halt or accelerate."[33]

In his first few months, Whitlam had several diplomatic achievements, such as opening Australia's doors to China and even Vietnam. This was an interesting feat since Australia had sent troops to fight in Vietnam not long before. Whitlam actually oversaw the final remnants of Australian troops be removed from Vietnam.

Gough Whitlam took note of the protest movement and decided to go even further than that. He heeded the calls of the youth and completely got rid of the military draft. He also made them happy by getting rid of fees to attend college.

Whitlam and his party spent quite a bit of money to create new and attractive social programs. Some of his contemporary critics, as well as critics today, might decry that these programs are nothing more than a bit of political chicanery to conjure up votes by giving free handouts to constituents.

Even though such things might have been incredibly appealing at the time, they were rather short-sighted. The Australian public would learn

---

[33] Blainey, Geoffrey. *A Shorter History of Australia*. 1994. Pg. 221.

that nothing was truly free. Shifting money from one place to another just created a different kind of financial burden. These efforts—no matter how popular they might have been—only helped to add to the ever-increasing level of inflation. It might have been a noble effort to funnel money into social welfare programs to help the poor, but if these same programs make the price of bread go through the roof by way of inflation, they really are not helping anyone in the long run.

Nevertheless, there were many who felt that such programs were needed, not only for the uplifting of citizens but also for the conservation of the environment. During this period, great conservation efforts were made. Large sections of the Outback were converted into national parks.

There was also a growing awareness of just how fragile Australia's environment could be. In 1983, a terrible spate of wildfires erupted. These fires led to the deaths of around seventy-five people and were extremely taxing on Australian rescue services. Wildfires continue to be a major problem for Australians to this day.

Vital national resources were being discovered in the meantime. For example, huge diamond deposits were found in the vicinity of Kimberly in Western Australia. There were also discoveries of oil and natural gas, which were soon being pumped into huge pipelines all the way to Perth.

Sizeable grants were put together for the sake of preserving old buildings deemed to have some sort of historical significance. Along with setting aside land for national parks and preserving historic buildings, the Australian government also established large tracts of land for the Aboriginals by allocating large portions of the Northern Territory to them.

There was a resurgence of Australian nationalism during this time. In many ways, it would perhaps be better to describe it as the discovery of Australian nationalism. Australia was so linked to Britain for much of its history that any sense of patriotism was a British sense of patriotism. But now Australians were suddenly trying to find themselves. The Australians discarded old distinctions in favor of new, entirely Australian ones. The Order of Australia was created to award extraordinary Australian citizens with an entirely Australian honor. This prestigious award is available to any Australian citizen who has proven themselves by performing some form of outstanding service or achievement.

These nationalistic overtures continued to take hold even in the midst of (and perhaps in spite of) an immigration boom that took off in the 1980s. Many immigrants came from Vietnam. Ever since the end of the war in Vietnam, several waves of people, who were often derisively dubbed the "boat people," showed up on Australian shores. It is estimated that by the year 1985, eighty thousand Vietnamese had come to Australia. By 2011, that number had increased to 180,000.

Vietnam was not the only part of the world that saw a massive influx of refugees head to Australia. The Lebanese Civil War, which lasted from 1975 to 1990, prompted quite a few refugees to seek a safer place to live. Most of these refugees were Greek Orthodox and Maronite Catholic, although some were also of the Muslim faith. No matter their religious background, all were seeking an escape from violence.

Chinese dissidents also sought asylum in Australia in the late 1980s. Many Chinese students were already in Australia on student visas when the Tiananmen Square protest occurred in China in 1989. During this infamous protest/revolt, a large group of mostly college-aged students tried to stand up to the communist government of China. Many communist regimes were falling apart in Eastern Europe during this time, and it seemed that these Chinese protesters were seeking a similar scenario in China. But that is not what happened.

The Chinese government cracked down with fury, and the protesters were met with machine guns and tanks. In consideration of the safety of the Chinese dissidents already in Australia on student visas, the Australian government agreed to allow many of these student visas to be converted into residential visas so that these students could effectively stay in Australia and remain safe from China's wrath.

Interestingly enough, in that same fateful year of 1989, Australia first went online. Australia was linked to the internet for the first time by way of the Australian Academic Research Network, which connected the University of Melbourne across the Pacific all the way to the University of Hawaii. Back in those days, the internet was largely used by universities for research purposes. This particular linkup was just the first step in Australia's internet usage.

Australia was rapidly changing, but even so, in 1988, a special bicentennial was held to celebrate two hundred years since the first Anglo settlers had arrived. This was celebrated on January 26th, 1988, to mark the two-hundredth anniversary of Captain Arthur Phillip's landing and the founding of the Australian colony of New South Wales. The Aboriginals of Australia decided that this date would be more aptly described as a day of mourning rather than anything to celebrate since it marked the end of their cultural dominance of the continent.

In many ways, Australians are still in the process of finding themselves. In a land of such diverse backgrounds and points of view, it is indeed hard to define exactly what it means to be Australian. In the 1980s, the *Mad Max* and *Crocodile Dundee* films tried to identify Australia with the rugged Outback and rugged masculinity.

Australia, unfortunately, was lambasted with more than its fair share of unintentional stereotypes. In August 1980, an Australian woman by the name of Lindy Chamberlain claimed that a dingo took her baby from her while she had been camping with her baby. She reportedly exclaimed, "A dingo's got my baby!"

The press ate it up, and Lindy was steadfastly disbelieved and roundly ridiculed. Some thought perhaps she had done something to the child and made up a goofy story about a dingo to cover it up. She was ultimately charged with the baby girl's murder and spent time in prison before the authorities realized that she was telling the truth. In 1986, the police discovered the child's bloody clothing in a dingo's nesting grounds. It was truly tragic what Lindy had to go through, both losing a child and being falsely accused of her child's demise. She and Australians as a whole also had to endure the stereotypical laughter of non-Australians asking them in a fake Australian accent, "So, did the dingo get your baby?"

The joke was still being used in the early 1990s; even the show *Seinfeld* used the line as a joke. Elaine mocked an Australian character in one episode. Apparently annoyed by the Australian, Elaine threw her off balance by suddenly proclaiming, "Maybe the Dingo ate your baby!"

This moment became iconic, but it was still a sad bit of stereotyping all the same. And the search for what it really meant to be an Australian—all mockery aside—would continue in full force. This search for national discovery was done by both European transplants and the descendants of Aboriginal people groups.

In the 1990s, Labor Prime Minister Paul Keating took a historic step in recognizing Aboriginal land rights with the passage of the Native Title Act. This landmark law, passed in December 1993, set up tribunals to determine which lands in Australia could be rightfully claimed by Aboriginal and Torres Strait Islander peoples.

The results were significant. Large portions of Australia's landmass were found to have potential Native title claims, sparking heated debates between Indigenous groups, farmers, and mining companies. However, while some early estimates suggested that over half of the continent could be subject to claims, many areas, such as private property and developed land, were excluded.

By 1998, more than seven hundred claims had been filed as Indigenous groups sought to reclaim their heritage and connection to their country. However, the process was slow, complex, and often frustrating. Many claims took years to resolve, requiring extensive historical, cultural, and legal proof to be recognized.

Much of the land under the Native claim was remote, rugged, and difficult to develop, but for Indigenous Australians, these places remained deeply significant. Even today, vast stretches of the Australian Outback remain uninhabited, not because of Native title claims but because of the harsh conditions and isolation.

There was a significant backlash among more conservative-leaning Australians in the meantime. They felt that the Australian government was going too far in appeasing Aboriginal rights groups. They found their voice in a populist political figure named Pauline Hanson. She was first elected to Parliament as an independent in 1996. She pushed back against some of the growing trends of multiculturalism and calls for Aboriginal rights. She decried what she described as government handouts to Aboriginals and claimed that Australians of European descent were being discriminated against in favor of benefiting minority groups such as the Aboriginals.

Pauline Hanson is a complicated figure, with some denouncing her as a narrow-minded bigot and others believing that she was a realist who was not afraid to speak her mind. In her opening speech in Parliament, she described herself as the ultimate outsider. She stated that she was just an everyday Australian woman seeking to make her nation better. Her critics, of course, never bought into this.

The modern era of Australia could be said to have truly begun under the leadership of Australian Prime Minister John Howard. He was elected prime minister in 1996 and served until 2007. He presided over a

John Howard.[20]

powerful Liberal-National Party coalition. This coalition instituted massive legislation for gun control and industry. They also overhauled taxation.

Not all of these measures were popular with everyone. At the start of John Howard's time as prime minister, tensions erupted into one of the most chaotic protests in Australian political history. On August 19th, 1996, thousands of union workers and Indigenous activists gathered outside Parliament House in Canberra, rallying against Howard's industrial relations policies and cuts to Indigenous programs.

What began as a peaceful demonstration soon spiraled out of control. A group of protesters stormed the front entrance, forcing their way into the Parliament House foyer and clashing with police. In the chaos, sixty police officers were injured, and fifty protesters were arrested.

A year after this dramatic unrest, populist parliamentarian Pauline Hanson managed to establish a political party of her own making, the One Nation Party. The group was popular and soon had members in excess of twenty-five thousand. In the 1998 election, the One Nation Party won nearly a quarter of the vote.

John Howard and his party were beset with questions about Australia's future identity as a governing entity. One of the more frequent questions was about when Australia would completely cut its links with Britain. Even though Australia was ostensibly independent and fully capable of handling its own affairs, the British monarch was still technically considered the head of state. As of this writing, Britain still has a say over the governor-general, who is appointed to represent the British monarch.

Howard created some trouble in 2001 when he appointed an Anglican archbishop to the role of governor-general. This selection was problematic for a variety of reasons. For one, many disagreed with having a bishop in the role due to the Australian notion of separation of church and state. More trouble erupted when it was revealed that the bishop had overseen investigations into previous sex abuse incidents in the church and had not handled it well. Hollingworth ultimately resigned in May 2003, becoming the first governor-general in Australian history to step down due to scandal.

Big changes were on the way later that year. Terrorists decided to strike multiple targets in the United States. The World Trade Center was destroyed in New York, and the Pentagon was badly damaged when terrorists hijacked planes and flew them into the targets. A third target was averted when passengers took matters into their own hands and attempted to storm the cockpit. The terrorists ended up taking the plane down in an empty field in Pennsylvania as a result. The passengers were killed, but they went down as heroes since they had thwarted the terrorists. It is widely believed that the terrorists who had hijacked this plane intended to send it crashing into either the US Capitol building or perhaps even the White House itself.

That fateful day in September day led to the War on Terror. Under George W. Bush, the American government was ready to exact vengeance, and their strategic partner Australia did not hesitate to lend a hand. The United States, after all, had suffered what seemed to be an entirely unprovoked attack (although some die-hard idealogues might try to argue that point), and most Australians were rather enthusiastic to show their support.

Australians would be involved in the subsequent US-led invasion of Afghanistan, which occurred as a result of the 9-11 attack. Afghanistan was not chosen at random. The Taliban regime of Afghanistan had sheltered and shielded the terrorist group al-Qaeda, which had orchestrated the attacks on the US. Immediately after the attack, the Bush administration demanded that the Taliban turn over the al-Qaeda terrorists who were responsible, and they refused. This was considered more than enough reason to launch a war against the Taliban regime.

Australian forces operating in Uruzgan during the War on Terror.[21]

The goal was to root out the terrorists, punish the Taliban, and attempt a regime change. After the disastrous pullout of US troops under President Joe Biden in 2021, some twenty years after the Taliban had initially been dismantled, all of these efforts came to naught since a resurgent Taliban resumed control of this troubled region.

At any rate, as it pertains to Australia's efforts in 2001, Australian armed forces were on the ground in Afghanistan, along with British and American troops. Shortly thereafter, US President Bush decided to up the ante by declaring that other countries could face preemptive strikes if it was believed they were harboring terrorist cells. Essentially, he was alluding to a potential strike against Iraq.

Australian Prime Minster Howard also began to speak in a very similar manner. He suggested that Australia should intervene in another country's affairs if they were found to be somehow harboring terrorists. This stance would be significantly challenged on October 12th, 2002, when a terrorist group bombed a nightclub in Bali in nearby Indonesia. This attack left eighty-eight Australians dead. Would Australia go to war with Indonesia?

Such a thing would be unthinkable. An Australian-Indonesian war would be devastating for both parties, as well as the surrounding region. Fortunately, it did not come to that since the Indonesian government was entirely forthcoming and cooperative in helping to hunt down the terrorists. As such, regime change was never on the menu in this instance.

This was not the case in Sadam Hussein's case, though. That is not to say that Sadaam was actually harboring terrorists or (as he was also accused) weapons of mass destruction in Iraq. However, Saddam was notoriously combative and non-cooperative with international inspectors. His combative nature seemed to lend credence to many of the Bush administration's accusations. Despite the United Nations attempting to dissuade Bush, the United States launched an invasion of Iraq in 2003.

The Australians, perhaps against their better judgment, stood next to their American allies and took part in this military operation as well. Australian soldiers were there along with American and British troops in March 2003 when the regime of Saddam Hussein was toppled. These allies later found that Saddam did not have weapons of mass destruction, and any supposed links to terrorism remained as dubious as ever. However, Australia did not get the same kind of blame as America and Britain did. America and Britain were seen as the leading antagonists, while Australia appeared to simply be backing them up. Howard had voiced doubt early on and was never wholeheartedly sold on the weapons of mass destruction.

Nevertheless, Australia remained on good terms with the United States. Things were so good that the two nations signed the Australia-United States Free Trade Agreement in 2004.

Interestingly, Howard weighed in on a presidential election in the United States. In 2007, he made some rather pointed remarks about Barack Obama's candidacy. Obama, who made the Iraq War a big part of his campaign, had spoken of his desire to withdraw US troops from Iraq if he was elected. As soon as Howard heard about this campaign pledge, he cried foul. He declared that such a move would be nothing short of surrender and that al-Qaeda was no doubt rooting for Obama to win the election due to his defeatist sentiment.

Obama did not take the criticism lightly. Around 140,000 US troops were in the region at the time, while Australia only had 1,400 soldiers. Obama suggested that if the Australian prime minister was so eager to continue the war, then he should go ahead and send another twenty thousand Australian soldiers into the war. Prime Minister Howard was unable to meet this challenge.

The long-running Howard government ultimately came to an end in 2007. It was succeeded by Prime Minister Kevin Rudd's government. Rudd helped steer Australia through an economic crisis in 2008. Because of his stewardship, Australia survived the storm. According to data on the subject, Australia fared better than many other countries.

Rudd also addressed the long-standing issue of Aboriginal rights, making it a point to actually go on the record and apologize for past government abuses toward Aboriginal peoples. He especially sought to address the matter of stolen generations, seeking to find forgiveness for the injustices of the past.

Prime Minister Rudd was in charge until 2013, when he was replaced by Tony Abbott. Abbott was replaced by political firebrand Malcolm Turnbull in 2015. Turnbull's government placed a heavy emphasis on relations with China. Turnbull was mainly concerned with Chinese aggression and competitiveness in the South China Sea. Turnbull also turned a wary eye toward Chinese 5G networks being installed in Australia. These Chinese 5G companies were ultimately banned.

Turnbull was out by 2018, and Scott Morrison took charge of Australia's government. Under the Morrison administration, Australia entered into the AUKUS agreement in the fall of 2021. AUKUS is short for "Australia, the United Kingdom, and the United States." This agreement was spearheaded by US President Joe Biden and sought to shore up strategic ties between the United States, the United Kingdom, and Australia to defend the whole Indo-Pacific region.

The initiation of the partnership immediately ignited controversy. Predictably enough, China did not appreciate the move, declaring that the efforts were essentially warmongering and harboring a "Cold War" mentality. But perhaps a bit less predictably, the initiative was also condemned by a Western ally—France.

The French were upset because the US pledged to build nuclear submarines for Australia as part of the deal. The French government felt as if it were thrown under the bus here since it had already contracted with the Australians to build submarines. This sudden change of plans meant the Australians canceled a deal with the French that was reportedly worth as much as ninety billion US dollars.

The French were not only upset that they had lost all of this potential revenue; they were also upset that they were given very little, if any, warning that such a deal was even in the works. This lack of cooperation between the signatories of AUKUS and France was condemned by the French foreign minister, Jean-Yves Le Drian, as nothing short of a stab in the back.

The French were not placated until Prime Minister Morrison was replaced by Anthony Albanese in Australia's 2022 election. Albanese finally settled the matter by agreeing to pay French contractor Naval Group hundreds of millions of dollars in compensation for the scrapped deal with France.

China continues to cast a wary eye on AUKUS and the Indo-Pacific partnership. For China, it is a clear challenge. In particular, it is believed that Australia's acquisition of nuclear-powered submarines would be used as a deterrent in the advent of a Chinese attempt to invade Tawain. Australia is a few thousand miles south of Tawain. That may seem like a good bit of distance, but Australia is certainly much closer than the other two members of AUKUS. Australia and its new nuclear subs one day may be placed on the front lines of a war with China.

China may be frustrated with such a prospect, but segments of Australia are worried about it as well. One dissenting voice, former Deputy Secretary of Defense Hugh White, made remarks in 2024, describing the deal as being fraught with danger for Australia.

White seems to be concerned that Australia will fall into the same old subservient trap that it faced with the British. Certain segments of Australia do not want the nation to be entirely submissive to the interests of a greater power and forced to fight its battles, especially if the conflict goes against Australia's own national interests.

Did the Australians really shake out of the grasp of Britain just to do the bidding of the United States? The implications are indeed huge. And in consideration of much, it remains to be seen what the future holds for Australia, AUKUS, the whole region, and the entire planet.

The phrase "World War Three" has been bandied about in recent years, especially in regard to hotspots such as Eastern Europe and the Middle East. However, the Indo-Pacific region is another flashpoint that could quickly flare up into an all-out global war. As of early 2025, there is still some semblance of peace in the waters surrounding Australia in the Indo-Pacific, but as political and international challenges continue to mount, there is no guarantee that this will remain the case indefinitely.

Conclusion: Australia's Future Foreign Policy

Australia has overcome more than its fair share of challenges. From the beginning, Australian settlers learned to get by in what was a harsh and often hostile environment. They built a robust nation that could stand tall among its global competitors. Australia served with distinction in two world wars and has since played a pivotal part in global affairs.

Most recently, Australia faced a foe that was both formidable and unexpected. Australia was deeply affected by the 2020 pandemic, just like much of the rest of the world. However, Australia showed firm resolve and managed to mitigate the dreaded virus. While much of the rest of the world was reeling from the effects of the coronavirus, Australia was able to undertake measures that greatly reduced the incidence of the disease. Both Australia and nearby New Zealand led the world in recovering from this terrible pandemic.

As much as Australia has been made to follow in the steps of other world powers, such as Britain and the United States, there is an increasing desire for Australia to be able to lead in its own right. The recent AUKUS partnership has seemingly doused gasoline on this passion, resulting in further cries for Australia to take greater hold of its own destiny.

However, for all of this wishful thinking, there are still plenty of pragmatic realists in Australia who realize that the Indo-Pacific region, in which Australia resides, may not always be the friendliest neighborhood.

Australia learned this lesson well enough during World War II when the Japanese landed right in Papua New Guinea.

If the Japanese had won the war, there is little doubt that Australia's future under Japanese hegemony would have been rather grim. Now, there are similar fears about the rising power of China. If there is a war over Tawain, would Australia be left in the middle of it? Or worse, would Australia and its nuclear submarines, courtesy of AUKUS, be forced to fight a war for the United States in an apocalyptic clash of superpowers?

As it pertains to the nation's march into the future, Australia will soon face an incredibly daunting foreign policy fork in the road. Should Australia exert more independent strategic actions? Or should it continue to toe the line in the name of collective security?

There are no easy answers to these questions, and arguments could be raised to support either side of the debate. Australia has always been in a unique position and has long played a unique role in world affairs. This important outpost will undoubtedly continue to be of great importance in the near future.

Part 2: Aboriginal Mythology

Enthralling Myths, Legends, and Folktales from Ancient Australia

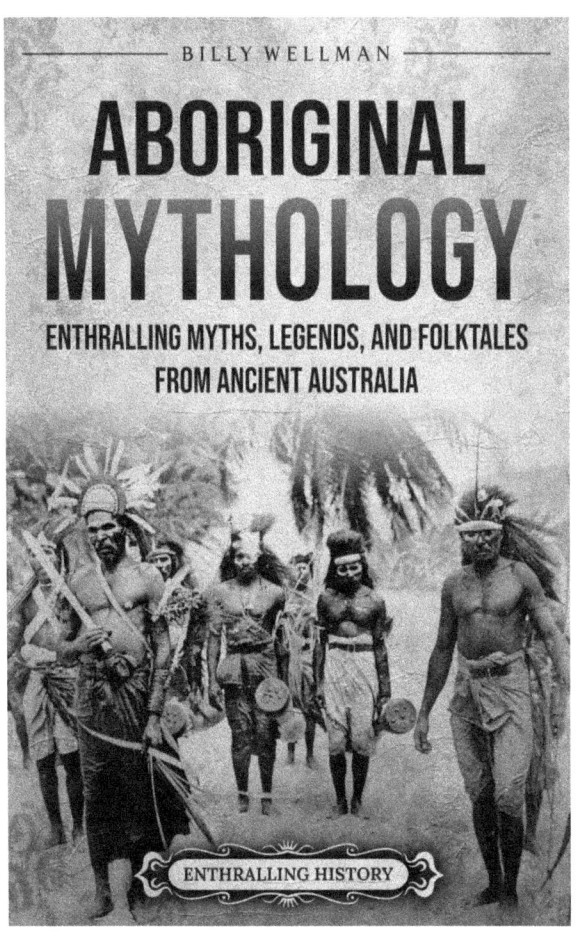

Introduction

Aboriginal mythology has been handed down through generations. These stories are far more than just entertainment; they are the stories of one of the world's oldest living cultures.

These narratives do more than narrate the dawn of time. They serve as lessons, moral compasses, and a means of connection to every aspect of the Aboriginal people's surroundings—from the tiniest grain of sand to the expansive heavens. Central to these tales is the Dreamtime, which represents the start of existence and whose spirits continue to shape the world.

Map of Aboriginal people's regions in Australia.[23]

Australia's landscape is as diverse as its stories, stretching from the red sands of the desert to the lush green of the rainforests to the deep blues of the ocean. This land has nurtured hundreds of Aboriginal nations, each with its own unique language, traditions, and stories.

With such a variety of cultures and communities, it is no wonder that the stories vary so much from one place to another. In one region, you might hear about the Rainbow Serpent, a powerful being that shapes the land and controls the water. Travel elsewhere, and the serpent's story changes.

These tales and stories are often filled with characters and symbols that might seem fantastical at first glance. They are filled with ancestral beings, talking animals, and forces of nature personified. However, they are more than just characters in a story. They represent deep connections to the land and to each other. Their tales talk about where to find water, how to read the stars, and the ways animals move with the seasons or even their breeding months.

The stories you will encounter are more than just historical artifacts. They are living lessons on sustainability, community, and the sacredness of the natural world. They challenge us to consider our impact on the earth and inspire us to forge deeper connections with the land.

A respectful reminder to Aboriginal and Torres Strait Islander readers: This book includes references to and images of people who have passed away.

Chapter 1: Dreamtime Creation Myths

It all began with nothing. It all started in the Dreamtime.

Before the clock began to tick and before the first calendar pages were turned, there existed a magical and mysterious period known as the Dreamtime. Dreamtime is like a mythological period of time in which life and the entire world came into being.

There isn't just one narrative that talks about how the earth and its inhabitants came to be; instead, there are many stories, reflecting the vast array of Aboriginal peoples and their deep connections to the land and its spirit. Some traditions tell of the earth's creation by gods of the Dreamtime, while others recount how specific animals, plants, and features of the landscape were brought into existence by different gods or ancestral spirits.

For several Aboriginal peoples of southeastern Australia, there was a very special celestial being known as Baiame. Baiame was a creator god, a powerful being who came down from the sky to shape the earth during the Dreamtime.

A painting by the Wonnarua depicting Baiame located near Milbrodale (to the south of Singleton, New South Wales).[38]

From his seat in the heavens, Baiame looked down upon the world, which was in complete darkness. What he saw was nothing else except a vast emptiness. There were no mountains standing tall, no rivers winding through the land, no trees swaying in the breeze, and no animals scurrying or soaring. The earth was silent and still.

Baiame decided it was finally time to create. He descended from the sky, touching the ground with the tips of his toes. Where his feet touched, the earth bloomed and came alive. Mountains rose up, reaching for the sky, and valleys emerged.

Next, the creator god sang, his melody weaving through the air, helping to give life to his surroundings. Rivers burst forth from the ground, dancing their way across the land. Then, trees sprouted up, reaching their branches high as if to catch the notes of Baiame's song. Flowers bloomed miraculously, filling the earth with a burst of vibrant colors.

The job was not yet done. Baiame knew the world would never be complete without creatures to roam, swim, and fly across it. So, with his divine abilities, he created a collection of animals and scattered them around the world. The kangaroo hopped across the plains, the emu strode through the grasslands, and the koala found its home among the branches of the gum trees (also known as eucalyptus trees). Fish filled the rivers, and birds flapped their wings in the skies. All kinds of creatures filled the land.

Baiame looked upon his creation with a smile.

"It is almost complete," he said.

The divine being moved on to his next creation. After gathering the dust of the earth, he carefully molded the first humans. He breathed life into them and taught them to live in harmony with the land. He showed them how to make shelters to protect themselves from nature and how to care for one another. Of course, Baiame also taught them the most important tool of survival: how to find food and water.

The first two humans gave birth to children, and their children gave birth to their own sons and daughters.

Baiame was generous. He gave much knowledge to the humans, ensuring that they could not only survive but also progress. However, he had one rule.

"You may eat these plants to sustain yourselves. But not the animals that I have created," Baiame said.

The grateful humans abided by his law. They lived in harmony with the earth and each other, just as the creator god had instructed them. That was the case until they were forced to face Mother Nature's wrath about a year later.

Mount Yengo, situated in the Wollombi Ranges near Awaba (Lake Macquarie), New South Wales, Australia. It stands solitary in the landscape. It is said that after Baiame completed the creation of the earth, he returned to the spirit world by leaping from this mountain, which he flattened in the process."

The earth began to change, and the seasons turned unpredictable. Fierce storms swept across the land, causing the humans to remain in their shelters. Then came the extreme drought. Crops failed, and the forests that had once teemed with life now whispered of hunger and despair. The people, once nurtured by the abundance Baiame had gifted them, found themselves struggling to survive in a world that seemed to have turned against them.

In desperation and perhaps guided by necessity, one man decided to break the harmony Baiame had taught them to cherish. The man, who was accompanied by his wife, hunted and killed a kangaroo. Some of the animal's flesh was offered to one of their friends, who was visibly losing weight due to the lack of food and drink. However, much to their surprise, their friend refused the meat despite being sick from hunger. The man remembered Baiame's warning, and after continuously refusing the offer, he rose to his feet and walked away.

Confused, the husband and wife gave only a shrug before continuing to enjoy their meal. Once they were done, their friend's actions began to weigh on their minds. Had they said something to offend him? Or was there some hidden message in what he did that they were meant to decipher? The more they pondered, the more their curiosity grew. The couple decided to go and check on their friend, hoping they could persuade him to finally eat.

After packing some food with them, the two went on their way. They carefully followed his trail, which led them to a river. They saw their friend lying under a tall gum tree across the river. The husband and wife wanted to reach him, but the stream was too swift for them to wade or even swim across. They wondered how their friend even managed to cross the river.

Suddenly, the couple saw a black figure emerging from the branches of the tree right above their friend. They squinted their eyes to get a better look at the figure, and they were stricken by horror at what they saw. The creature appeared to be half-man, half-beast. Panicked, the husband and wife shouted to warn their friend, who was still sleeping under the tree. However, their friend was unable to hear them; he wouldn't have been able to hear them even if he were wide awake. The creature picked up the man, who was still not moving, and carried him into the branches, disappearing from sight.

From there on, a few more mysterious events took place. A burst of smoke shot out from the very same gum tree where their friend was resting. The couple kept on watching, their hearts pounding rapidly, as the tree began to move. It was as if the tree had come alive, lifting itself off the ground, roots snapping like twigs. The tree then soared across the river, flying south. As it glided by, the husband and wife spotted something even more chilling: two menacing, bright eyes peeking out from the shadows of the tree and two white cockatoos, flapping their wings wildly as if trying to catch up with the flying tree, which had possibly been their shelter all this time.

Before they knew it, the tree, the cockatoos, and those eerie glowing eyes had become just a tiny dot in the distance, far away to the south and high up in the sky. The husband and wife were made to realize that they had witnessed, for the first time, the event of death. The creature that they saw was Yowi, the spirit of death.

Just a few moments ago, he was seen alive. The next minute, he was dead, just like the kangaroo that had been killed for food by the husband and wife. All living things mourned upon learning of what had happened to the man.

This story, drawing particularly from the lore of the Kamilaroi (also spelled as Gamileroi or Kamilroi) tribe, narrates a profound moment when death is introduced to the world created by Baiame, the creator god. The tale is rich with symbolism and carries deeper meanings related to the cycles of life and death, the balance of existence, and the relationship between humans, nature, and the spiritual realm.

Another prominent Dreamtime story that tells the creation of the world comes from the Kamilaroi tribe. This narrative also begins with a description of how, in the beginning, there was only darkness as the world was asleep, waiting for a certain spark to ignite the dawn of creation. This spark came in the form of Yhi, a being of light and life. Her deep slumber was disturbed by the sound of a mysterious whistle. Some stories also suggest that Yhi was awakened by Baiame. The moment Yhi's eyes fluttered open, light cascaded upon the earth for the first time, piercing the veil of darkness and introducing warmth to the cold, barren land.

However, that was only the beginning of the story. Wherever Yhi wandered, the ground beneath her feet was said to have burst into life. The earth was covered in verdant green. Yet, Yhi yearned for more than just the stillness of the fauna; she envisioned a world filled with movement and dance.

To fulfill this quest, she delved deep into the earth, where she encountered evil spirits that tried to overwhelm her with their sinister songs. More than once, they tried singing her to death. However, Yhi's radiance was too powerful, and her warmth dispelled the shadows. The malevolent spirits were transformed into a multitude of insects, which Yhi brought forth into the world.

Her journey did not end there. The creator discovered ice caves hidden within a mountain that had long become a shelter for slumbering creatures. With her light, she awakened these beings. Fishes slipped into the streams, lizards scurried into the sunlight, and the air was filled with all sorts of birds.

Her quest was complete. Having breathed life into the earth, Yhi returned to her celestial realm. Before she left, she gave her creations the gift of seasons—a cycle of life, death, and rebirth—as well as a promise to place her creations among the stars when their time on Earth ended.

However, her departure brought darkness once more. The creatures, fearing Yhi's absence was permanent, mourned her loss. Thankfully, their sorrow was short-lived. For with the dawn came the first sunrise—a daily reminder of Yhi's presence and the promise of her return.

As time passed by, the animals began to grow restless. Yhi heeded their call. She descended from the heavens to hear their desires. First, she listened to the kangaroo who wished for the freedom to leap. Then, she listened to the wombat who yearned to burrow in the earth. The seal wanted to swim. The lizard told the creator about his wish to have legs to roam the land, and the bat told her of his dream of having wings to explore the skies. The platypus wished for a bit of everything. Yhi granted their wishes.

Yhi noticed that man was unlike any other creature she had fashioned. She also noticed the man's loneliness in the vast world. As he slept, Yhi focused all her energy on a single flower, imbuing it with her essence. The next morning, the man awoke to find the companionship of animals and a woman, who had been born from the flower.

Yhi had ensured that every creature had a place and a partner. With her task now done, Yhi ascended to the sky once more, her heart content.

Chapter 2: Songlines and Their Spiritual Significance

In the past, Aboriginal people did not rely on compasses or even stars to navigate the land. Instead, they relied on songlines that serve as invisible threads that link the physical world to the spiritual world. Each songline is a lyrical pathway, charting routes across the land and the sky through verses that tell stories of landmarks, waterholes, and sacred sites.

The origin of songlines is rooted deep in the Aboriginal creation stories known as the Dreamtime. Ancestral beings traversed the barren, formless land. As they moved, they sang the world into existence, their voices calling forth mountains, rivers, plants, and animals. These songs did not just shape the physical features of the landscape but also laid down the pathways that their descendants would follow.

Imagine for a moment that you were an Aboriginal traveler living thousands of years ago. To navigate the continent, you are equipped with not a physical map but songlines sung by the elders. These songs describe the landmarks you will see along your journey, from towering mountains to hidden springs. Each verse is a step, and each rhyme is a guide to the next landmark. By singing these songs, you can navigate vast distances, even through territories that you have never set foot in before.

It is crucial to follow these paths with respect and mindfulness. For Aboriginal people, the land is imbued with sacredness. A songline often dictates not just the path but also the direction in which it should be traveled. Deviating from this path or going in the wrong direction can be seen as disrespectful or even sacrilegious. A notable example is Uluru, the majestic sandstone monolith in the southern part of the Northern Territory, Central Australia.

Uluru is more than just a geological wonder. According to the Anangu, the traditional custodians of Uluru, this place is deeply embedded in the Dreamtime. The myths surrounding Uluru tell of ancestral beings who roamed the earth during creation. They shaped the landscape and created laws. Uluru is believed to be the physical evidence of their activities, making it a deeply sacred place where the earth's spiritual energy is palpable.

The ancestral stories associated with Uluru involve epic tales of battles, with features of the rock thought to be the marks left behind by these beings. For the Anangu, every crevice, cave, and natural formation on Uluru has a story. Ceremonies and rites are performed there to maintain the harmony between the spiritual and physical worlds.

Recognizing the sacredness of Uluru and in response to the longstanding wishes of the Anangu people, climbing on Uluru was officially banned in October 2019. For decades, the Anangu had requested visitors not to climb Uluru, as doing so was seen as a desecration of a sacred space. The act of climbing not only disrespected traditional laws and beliefs but also posed a physical risk to the climbers and caused environmental damage to this precious site. The ban on climbing Uluru represents a significant step toward recognizing and honoring the cultural rights and spiritual practices of Aboriginal Australians.

The sacred Uluru.[25]

Songlines vary throughout Australia, reflecting the unique geography, flora, fauna, and cultural significance of each region.

- **The Yolngu People of Arnhem Land:** They recount the journey of Barnumbirr, a creator-being symbolized by the planet Venus. Originating from the island of Baralku in the east, Barnumbirr is celebrated for guiding the first humans to Australia. As she flew from east to west, Barnumbirr named and created the landscape's features. Her journey across the sky at dawn is still seen as a guide for the Yolngu people, reminding them of the eternal link between their ancestors and the land.

- **The Yarralin People of the Victoria River Valley:** They venerate Walujapi, the Dreaming Spirit of the black-headed python. Walujapi carved a snakelike track along a cliff face. The impression of her buttocks, which were left as she established camp, is a sacred site.

- **In the Sydney Region:** With valleys often ending abruptly in canyons or cliffs, the ridge lines become natural pathways. Songlines in this area predominantly follow these ridges, where the journey is easier and where sacred art, including the Sydney rock engravings, is found. This contrasts with other parts of Australia, where songlines might meander through valleys, drawn toward water sources and the sustenance they promise.

The Wirangu and the Seven Sisters Creation Story

For generations, the Wirangu people have been the heart and soul of the wild western coast of South Australia. They are the land's traditional custodians. The Wirangu people's heritage, passed down through countless generations, speaks of their deep relationship with this place, where the fierce ocean hits the rugged cliffs and reaches inland to the desert sands.

The Wirangu people's understanding of the world around them is deeply embedded in their language and cultural practices, which honor the land as a living entity. Every element of the natural world holds significance, from the smallest grain of sand to large boulders, as each carries stories from the Dreamtime.

The arrival of European settlers in the 1800s marked the beginning of a tumultuous period for the Wirangu. This era brought a wave of dispossession, cultural disruption, and a decline in population. The settlers, driven by a desire to claim and cultivate the land, often failed to recognize the sacredness of the earth and the intricate ties that bound the Wirangu to their ancestral territories.

One of the most harrowing episodes of this period was the events that unfolded around Elliston and Streaky Bay. In 1849, at least twenty-five Wirangu people, along with members of other Indigenous groups, were driven from the cliffs at Elliston to their deaths in the ocean below. For years, the areas around Elliston and Streaky Bay became taboo.

Yet, the spirit of the Wirangu proved resilient. In recent years, efforts have been made to acknowledge this painful chapter of Aboriginal history. To honor the lives lost, a memorial was erected at Elliston in 2017 after consulting with the Wirangu and other Aboriginal communities. Today, the monument serves as a place for reflection and healing. People often gather there to pay their respects.

Central to this journey of reconnection is the Wirangu people's songline creation story involving the Seven Sisters or Kungkarangkalpa. This tale begins in the Dreamtime when the world was young and the spirits roamed the earth, shaping the land and imbuing it with life.

The Seven Sisters are ethereal beings in the sky who descended to the earth one day, bringing with them radiance and beauty that were unknown to the land below. Their appearance was said to ignite an insatiable desire among the men who witnessed them. Completely enchanted and overwhelmed by their beauty, these men decided to pursue the sisters, hoping they could make them their lifelong companions. However, the sisters used their digging sticks to repel these advances.

However, the narrative takes a turn with the introduction of Wati Nyiru, also known as Yurlu, a sorcerer. Yurlu's desire to take one of the sisters as his wife was thwarted by his skin color. He was not of the correct skin group, a crucial aspect of the Aboriginal tradition that governs social and marital relations to maintain harmony and prevent close genetic intermingling. Despite this, Yurlu's infatuation spurred him to follow the sisters, hoping to overcome any barriers.

Yurlu's pursuit was marked by determination and the use of sorcery and shapeshifting. He would bend the will of the cosmos to his desires. Even though he managed to capture one of the sisters at Pangkapini, the sisters escaped time and time again. The eldest of the sisters was said to have taught her siblings to transform themselves into trees. This was done so they could hide from Yurlu and rest.

Eventually, the sisters made their way from the sands of Pirilyi to the waterhole at Puyatu, where they sought refuge in a cave. Yurlu refused to let a moment pass without having both of his eyes on the sisters. He watched them from a distance, his presence marked today by a stone mound believed to represent Yurlu's figure spying on the Seven Sisters.

Knowing that Yurlu had his eyes on them, the sisters planned their escape. Instead of exiting out of the only entrance to the cave, the sisters used their digging sticks to dig out a secret hole at the back of the cave. Once they were done, the sisters quickly escaped, hoping they could lose Yurlu.

In a desperate act, Yurlu employed his sorcery once again. He sent his phallus, in the form of a carpet snake, to chase the Seven Sisters. The snake was said to have slithered across the vast land, attempting to locate the women. The Seven Sisters noticed the snake, though. Mistaking the creature for food, one of the sisters took the snake. Little did they know, Yurlu had been trailing the snake all this while and was a step closer to capturing the Seven Sisters.

However, the Seven Sisters realized the danger they were in and tossed the snake into the horizon before fleeing. And so, the pursuit resumed. As the Seven Sisters fled from Yurlu across the varied landscapes of Australia, their journey left an impact on the earth. With every step and leap, they shaped the world beneath their feet, creating the world as we know it today.

As they moved, the Seven Sisters used their digging sticks, creating craters and valleys. The natural features formed by the sisters' journey were more than geographical landmarks; they were places imbued with meaning. Their path, which cut across the territories of the Martu, Anangu, Pitjantjatjara, Yankunytjatjara, and Ngaanyatjarra peoples, wove a network of songlines that stretched across the continent.

The Seven Sisters ascended to the heavens, seeking refuge among the stars, and transformed into the Pleiades constellation. Yurlu refused to give up. The sorcerer followed the sisters to the sky, continuing the pursuit for eternity. Even today, we can see the Pleiades constellation being chased by the constellation Orion.

A widefield view of the Pleiades.[26]

Interestingly, the significance of the Seven Sisters' journey is not confined to Aboriginal Australian culture alone. The Pleiades constellation holds an important place in numerous cultures around the world. The ancient Greeks saw them as the daughters of the Titan Atlas and the Oceanid nymph Pleione, and the Native Americans interpreted the constellation's appearance as a sign to begin the harvest.

A one-dollar silver coin issued in 2020 by the Royal Australian Mint that features the Seven Sisters.[27]

Yurlu never gave up his pursuit. His desire propelled him upward. He, too, became a constellation.

Yurlu became Orion, which is one of the most recognizable constellations in the night sky. In many cultures, Orion is depicted as a hunter perpetually following the cluster of stars known as the Pleiades. The positioning of Orion and the Pleiades serves as a cosmic reenactment of the Dreamtime story, with the gap between them symbolizing both the physical distance and the cultural laws that keep Yurlu from achieving his desire.

Chapter 3: The Lore of the Rainbow Serpent

Serpents slither through myths and legends of cultures around the world, often embodying chaos and destruction. In Egyptian mythology, Apophis (also known as Apep) was a formidable force of chaos. This enormous serpent dwelled in the darkness of the underworld and perpetually thwarted the sun god Ra's journey during the night. This age-old story symbolizes the eternal struggle between order and chaos.

Farther north, in the cold realms of Norse mythology, lives Jörmungandr. Known as the World Serpent, this creature was born of the trickster god Loki and the giantess Angrboda. Jörmungandr is described to be extremely enormous. It encircles Midgard (the realm of humans) until it can bite its own tail. This monstrous serpent is fated to release its grip only at Ragnarök (the end of the world). When this time comes, Jörmungandr will emerge from the sea to poison the sky and battle the thunder god Thor, which will lead to their mutual destruction. Jörmungandr symbolizes the inevitable end of all things.

The Rainbow Serpent of Aboriginal mythology diverges significantly from these narratives of destruction. It is far from being a monstrous entity. The Rainbow Serpent is actually revered as a powerful creator being, a life-giver whose presence and actions were integral to the birth of the landscape and life itself.

The Rainbow Serpent as the Creator of Beings

The Rainbow Serpent is known by many names across the continent, such as Ngalyod by the Kunwinjku people of Arnhem Land, Borlung by the Miali people of the Northern Territory, and Goorialla by the Lardil people of Mornington Island. The difference in names reflects the multifaceted role the Rainbow Serpent plays across Australia. For the Kunwinjku, Ngalyod represents the dual nature of the serpent as both a giver and taker of life. Borlung highlights the serpent's power over rain and storms. The spirit could bring life to the land but was also capable of causing floods. For the Lardil, Goorialla symbolizes the serpent's journey across the land, shaping the rivers, hills, and valleys that dotted the landscape.

According to the Wiradjuri people, the story of creation begins with Baiame, the sky father and creator god, who sent the Rainbow Serpent to the earth. This celestial being's arrival marked the beginning of the transformation of a world that was once empty and flat. After emerging from underground, the Rainbow Serpent began its journey across the continent. With every movement, the Rainbow Serpent's body carved out the contours of the earth, creating mountains, rivers, and gorges.

As the Rainbow Serpent traversed the barren lands, it encountered beings that had yet to realize their purpose. The Rainbow Serpent realized there was a great need for water to nurture the lifeless earth, and it called upon the frogs. The Rainbow Serpent coaxed the frogs into releasing the waters they hoarded. As the frogs laughed and danced, water burst forth, filling the rivers and gorges carved by the Rainbow Serpent.

A rock painting of the Rainbow Serpent.[38]

From these waters, life sprang forth. Trees stretched their limbs toward the sky, their leaves capturing the light and casting shadows on the ground below. Flowers bloomed in vibrant hues. Animals of all kinds emerged, from the smallest insect to the largest mammal. The land, once silent and still, now teemed with the sounds of life.

With its task completed, the Rainbow Serpent grew tired. It was said to have slithered away, claiming his hard-earned rest.

The Rainbow Serpent is also credited with the creation of humans. According to one story, after breathing life into the animals of Australia, the Rainbow Serpent taught them to live in harmony with each other. But some refused to obey the serpent's will; they caused trouble and argued with each other.

"I will gladly turn those who lived by my laws into humans," the serpent said. "Those who disobeyed will be punished. You will be turned to stone and never walk this earth ever again."

The Rainbow Serpent followed through on his threat. Those who had sown discord and refused to live in harmony were transformed into stone. Their forms became the mountains and hills that dot the landscape, becoming eternal reminders of the consequences of disregarding the laws of harmony. Those creatures who embraced the Rainbow Serpent's teachings were elevated to human form. Each was bestowed with a totem reflecting their animal, bird, or reptile origins—kangaroo, emu, carpet snake, and others—marking their tribes and connecting them to the land.

This division of totems among the tribes was not arbitrary. By decreeing that no individual should consume the animal of their totem, the Rainbow Serpent created a system of mutual respect and interdependence. This ensured that no species would be overhunted, preserving the balance of the ecosystem.

The Rainbow Serpent as the Protector of Water

In the Kuninjku language of Arnhem Land (located in the Northern Territory), the Rainbow Serpent is known as Ngalyod, a being linked to water sources such as creeks and rivers. This ancestral spirit is responsible for the lush vegetation that thrives near water, including water lilies, vines, and palms.

The Rainbow Serpent's dwelling, believed by some Aboriginal cultures to be within waterholes, has to be approached with care to avoid invoking its wrath. While not inherently a creature of destruction, the Rainbow Serpent is capable of summoning storms, high winds, and rain. The

Indigenous people engage in a specific ritual to announce their presence and intentions to the Rainbow Serpent. By singing out to the Rainbow Serpent, they signal their knowledge of the place and their respect for the traditions connected to it.

Did you know?

Maraiin ceremonies are deeply revered and sacred events that span several days. They feature an intricate blend of song and dance. During these ceremonies, song men (a title for respected men who are keepers of the sacred stories and songs) perform narratives of the ancestral beings' heroic deeds. They are accompanied by the rhythmic beats of a clapstick player and a didgeridoo. The song cycles dedicated to the Rainbow Serpent are of great importance. The ceremonies also celebrate the Water Goanna, which is believed to have created waterholes across western Arnhem Land before transforming into a goanna. In a captivating display, large wooden effigies of the Rainbow Serpent and the Water Goanna are carried by dancers to the ceremonial ground. Here, participants mimic the movements of these revered figures, paying homage to their roles in the natural world and cultural heritage.

The people also take a handful of earth and rub it on their bodies, a gesture that allows the Rainbow Serpent to "smell" them. It is a way of showing that they come in peace with no intention to harm or disrespect the Rainbow Serpent's home. After these rituals are observed, the people can approach the waterhole to drink.

Goorialla, the Rainbow Serpent Who Tricked the Rainbow Lorikeet Brothers

The story of Goorialla, the Rainbow Serpent, is an integral part of Aboriginal Australian mythology. It specifically originates from the Dreamtime stories of the Northern Territory. The story has been popularized through children's literature, notably by authors Dick Roughsey and Percy Trezise, who adapted this Aboriginal tale into a format accessible to younger audiences.

Goorialla's tale begins with his departure from the southern regions of Australia. He was driven by a desire to locate his kin. As he moved northward, he molded the once flat and featureless land into hills, valleys, and waterways.

Goorialla was welcomed enthusiastically by his people. The people engaged in song and dance, which Goorialla observed with keen interest. However, he soon noted discrepancies in their ceremonial practices. After asserting his authority, Goorialla corrected their dances and attire, instructing them in the proper ways of performing a ceremony. This intervention highlights Goorialla's role not just as a creator of the physical world but also as a custodian of cultural knowledge and practices.

However, the joyful reunion was soon overshadowed by a formidable storm. As the community braced for the tempest, everyone sought shelter in hastily constructed humpies (a type of simple temporary shelter commonly built by the Aboriginals). Among them were the Bil Bil brothers, two rainbow lorikeet (a species of small, colorful parrots native to Australia) who found themselves without refuge. In their desperation, they approached Goorialla, who deceitfully promised them shelter. Goorialla actually swallowed the brothers whole.

Fearful of the consequences once the community realized the brothers had disappeared, Goorialla fled. The clan traced Goorialla's path to a mountain. The Goanna (an Australian monitor lizard) brothers undertook a daring rescue. Scaling the mountain, they found Goorialla asleep. They managed to free the Bil Bil brothers from his belly. The brothers, now transformed into birds, escaped.

Goorialla awoke to the sounds coming from his empty stomach. In his rage, Goorialla threw bits of the mountain across the landscape. These bits turned into the hills and mountains we see today. Some of the people wanted to evade Goorialla's wrath, and they transformed into various forms of wildlife. By the time his anger diminished, only a small part of the original mountain—the one he had once rested on—remained. He then slithered down the small hill and made his way into the sea, where he was believed to be to this day. The legend concludes with a reminder of the responsibility humans have toward the natural world, a world that was once populated by beings who now exist in the form of animals, birds, and insects.

Another version of the story focuses on the aftermath of Goorialla's actions. After swallowing the brothers, Goorialla ascended to the sky, the only place he believed he could be safe. From his celestial vantage point, Goorialla witnessed the profound sorrow of the people mourning the loss of the young men. Moved by their grief, he sought to atone for his actions.

Goorialla decided to transform his body into an arc of vibrant colors stretching across the sky. This transformation was his way of expressing remorse for taking the rainbow lorikeet brothers. In the moments following a rain shower, the Rainbow Serpent's colors can be seen in the sky. This appearance serves as Goorialla's apology.

Chapter 4: Aboriginal Constellations and Celestial Myths

The Aboriginal Australians have long held an important connection with the cosmos, telling stories as intricate as the constellations overhead.

For the Aboriginal people of Australia, the stars were not merely a spectacle of light in the dark sky; they were a map, a calendar, and a library of endless knowledge passed down through generations. Without the telescopes and gadgets that modern astronomers depend on, they had to understand the heavens above them. Doing so allowed them to predict when the seasons changed, when it was time to harvest, and when it was time to move.

They knew that when the emus in the sky run, it was the best time to hunt the creature and collect its eggs. When they caught a glimpse of the star Parna (Fomalhaut) in the morning, they knew that the annual autumn rains would arrive soon and that it was time for them to build large waterproof huts.

One Dreamtime story tells the origin of a certain constellation and a crater. This is the tale as recounted by Aunty Mavis Malbunka, the custodian of the Western Arrernte people of the Central Desert.

Long ago, in the Dreamtime, a group of women existed in the form of dazzling stars. With the Milky Way as their stage, they performed a corroboree, a sacred dance ceremony. The night sky became alive with their movements, as if there was a celestial ballet that celebrated creation. One of these women was a mother, and she brought her baby to this cosmic gathering. As she grew tired from the dance, the mother placed her child, cradled in a coolamon (a type of wooden basket or vessel), on the edge of the Milky Way. The mother then rejoined the other women.

The baby, perhaps stirred by the music of the cosmos or the gentle sway of the coolamon, slipped off the edge of the Milky Way and began tumbling toward the earth. The descent was silent, a falling star unnoticed against the backdrop of a billion others, until the baby and the coolamon struck the ground with great force.

This phenomenon formed a ring-shaped mountain range that is 5 kilometers wide and 150 meters high. This place, known to some as the Gosses Bluff Crater, is known by the Arrernte as Tnorala. To the Arrernte, this giant crater, formed over 140 million years ago by a cosmic event, hid the baby from the cosmos. Because of this, the baby's parents—the morning and evening stars—never reunited with their child. However, they never give up, and the search continues to this day.

Air view of Tnorala or the Gosses Bluff Crater.[39]

The Arrernte people hold this site in deep reverence, as it is a place where the veil between the earthly and the celestial realms is thin. Visitors are welcome to witness the site, but they have to be respectful. The story can also be seen in the winter sky; visitors may have a chance to see the constellation known as Corona Australis right below the Milky Way. Its arc of stars represents the falling coolamon.

The Corona Australis as seen by the naked eye.[80]

The Markers of Seasonal Change: Pleiades, Baidam, and Arcturus

Also known affectionately as the Seven Sisters—though many more stars comprise this cluster—the Pleiades are a sight to behold. It is nestled within the constellation of Taurus. The Pleiades begin their ascent in the dawn sky just as winter starts to announce its arrival. The sight of Pleiades is a prelude to the colder months that lie ahead.

To the naked eye, the star cluster appears as a delicate mist of light. Through the lens of a telescope, the Pleiades reveal their true splendor—each star is a fiery beacon with blue-white hues.

This star cluster has served as a guide and a symbol for the Aboriginal Australians for millennia. The appearance of the Pleiades heralds the peak of the dingo breeding season. To the Aboriginal people, dingoes are companions in the cold winter nights, a source of warmth, and, during times of scarcity, a source of nourishment.

The Pleiades.[81]

However, the significance of the Pleiades extends beyond the dingoes. The bush tomatoes (kutjera), honey ants (tjala), and thorny devils (mingari) are all linked through interrelated traditions and songlines to this star cluster.

Another important constellation takes the form of a shark. It is known as Baidam among the Torres Strait Islanders (one of Australia's two distinct Indigenous cultural groups). Since sharks play a crucial role in maintaining healthy marine ecosystems—they are apex predators that help control the populations of other species—Baidam is considered to have been a symbol of life and sustenance.

Baidam's form is outlined by the seven bright stars that make up the Big Dipper, which is part of the larger constellation Ursa Major. As Baidam makes its grand entrance into the night sky, it signals a time of abundance and renewal, a period when the Torres Strait Islanders prepare the soil for planting crops of sugarcane, sweet potato, and banana. When the nose of this celestial shark touches the horizon right after sunset, it marks the start of the shark breeding season.

To the west, in the traditions of the Wergaia people of Victoria, another story unfolds. In the heart of a land parched by drought, where the sun scorched the earth until it cracked, there lived a people on the brink of despair. Food was just a memory, and the rivers and billabongs (a body of water in Australia often formed when a river changes course) that once teemed with life were now silent. In these dire times, a woman named Marpeankurric rose.

Marpeankurric knew that surrendering to despair was not what her ancestors would do. She set forth into the wilderness, her eyes looking for any sign of food. Days melted into nights under the relentless sun, and the land offered nothing. However, Marpeankurric's resolve was as bright as the stars in the sky above her.

Finally, fortune finally smiled upon Marpeankurric. Hidden beneath the cracked earth, sheltered from the prying eyes of the sun, lay a nest of wood ants, which her people referred to as bittur. Marpeankurric unearthed the nest to reveal thousands of ant larvae, which were more precious than pearls. Without hesitation, Marpeankurric tasted the larvae, finding them not only edible but also surprisingly flavorful.

Marpeankurric hurried back to her people, her heart overjoyed. Because of Marpeankurric's courage, her people were saved, and the ant larvae became an essential food source during the winter months.

However, Marpeankurric's legacy did not end with her earthly journey. In recognition of her valor and the lives she saved, she was honored after she passed away. Marpeankurric ascended to the heavens, her essence immortalized as the bright star Arcturus.

Arcturus is a giant star in the Northern Hemisphere, and it is brightest in the evening sky from late spring to summer. To see Arcturus, one needs to gaze toward the west shortly after sunset, where it shines as the brightest star in the constellation of Boötes, the Herdsman. Its appearance signifies that it is time to harvest ant larvae.

Arcturus, the brightest star in the constellation of Boötes.[83]

Other Constellations and Their Significance

Constellation	Description	Narrative/Significance
Yurree and Wanjel	Represented by the stars Castor and Pollux in Gemini. Yurree is the fan-tailed cuckoo, and Wanjel is the long-necked tortoise.	These stars symbolize two hunters in pursuit of the kangaroo, Purra. Their appearance in the sky marks the cuckoo's activity season and the tortoise's egg-laying time.
Purra	Symbolized by the star Capella, representing the Red Kangaroo.	Purra appears in the sky from August to February. It is followed by two hunters, Yurree and Wanjel.
Warepil	Centered around Sirius, Warepil is the male wedge-tailed eagle. This figure is significant across Victoria.	Known as Bunjil in Melbourne, Warepil represents leadership and creation.
Neilloan	Vega is the anchor star for Neilloan, which depicts the malleefowl.	The constellation is visible in autumn mornings and disappears in spring evenings. This aligns with the malleefowl's nesting and egg-laying season.

Constellation	Description	Narrative/Significance
Brolgas	Illustrated by the Large and Small Magellanic Clouds (a pair of galaxies), these stars form the constellation of Kourtchin, showing a pair of dancing brolgas (a kind of bird).	Visible all year in Victoria's dark skies, this constellation celebrates the joyous dance of the brolgas.

The Story of the Evil Emu

At the dawn of creation, the great ancestor spirit Bunjil sculpted the world, giving birth to the majestic sandstone ranges of Gariwerd, also known as the Grampians. Transforming into Warepil the Eagle, Bunjil soared high, his eyes reflecting the beauty of his creations, from the whispering waterfalls to the towering gum trees.

Near the heart of Gariwerd, Bunjil found a place from where he could watch over the ranges. There, immortalized in Bunjil's Shelter, he stood with his faithful Wirringan, the dingoes who served as his eyes and ears. To bring order to this new world, Bunjil summoned the Bram-bram-bult brothers, children of Druk the Frog. Their task was to name the creatures, bestow languages, and lay down the laws that would govern everything.

As Bunjil ascended to the heavens, becoming a star that would forever watch over the land, a shadow loomed on the horizon. The emu Tchingal, a creature of darkness, roamed the mallee scrub. In its nest lay a colossal egg.

One day, Waa the Crow, driven by hunger, happened upon Tchingal's nest. The sight of the unguarded egg was too tempting. As Waa pecked at the shell, savoring the taste, Tchingal returned. The emu was enraged to see what was happening to its unborn baby. Waa quickly realized the gravity of the situation and took to the skies, fleeing toward the sanctuary of Gariwerd. Tchingal was hot on his trail, though.

As Waa approached the ranges, he spied a crack in the mountains. Darting into the crevice, he believed himself safe, but Tchingal struck the mountain with a force that shook the earth to its core. The mountain yielded, birthing Barigar, also known as Rose's Gap, and from its heart, a stream was born.

Tchingal pursued Waa through the newly formed gap. In a desperate bid for safety, Waa found another crevice, but again, Tchingal's might was unstoppable. Tchingal split the rock, creating Jananginj Njaui (Victoria Gap), where the Glenelg River escapes to the plains. As dusk embraced the land, Tchingal ended his pursuit, marking the place where the sun bids farewell. Jananginj Njaui means "the place where the sun will go."

The following morning, Waa sought refuge in Moora Moora swamp, a place sacred to him and where Tchingal's fury could not reach him. Yet, Tchingal's hunger for vengeance remained unquenched. It was then that Bunya, a man of the land, caught Tchingal's gaze. Bunya fled at the sight of the emu, abandoning his spears. Bunya climbed a tree, hoping for salvation among the branches. Tchingal waited below.

Word of Tchingal's evil reached the Bram-bram-bult brothers, who vowed to end the emu's reign of terror. Approaching under the guise of night, they found Tchingal. From the shadows, they launched their spears, striking Tchingal. Wounded, the emu fled toward the northern plains, its blood giving birth to the Wimmera River. Eventually, Tchingal died.

Bunya, still perched within the tree, hesitated to descend as fear clouded his judgment. In response to his cowardice, the elder brother transformed him into a possum, condemning him to a life among the treetops and seeking sustenance in the night.

The brothers then plucked Tchingal's feathers before splitting each of them down the center. They threw the split feathers, half to their right and the other half to their left. These two separate piles of emu feathers then transformed into the emus that we see today. Interestingly, the splitting of the feathers can still be seen on present-day emus; their feathers appear double with two separate halves.

Right before they moved on, the Bram-bram-bult brothers had to make sure no egg would ever spark such envy and strife again. They ordered the two new emus to divide their large egg into a few smaller ones.

In the heavens above, the story of Tchingal and the Bram-bram-bult brothers is etched among the stars. The Southern Cross, with Bunya at its head and the spears as its points, narrates the tale. Waa the Crow shines as Canopus.

The Southern Cross, also known as the Crux, as seen by the naked eye.[88]

Although Tchingal is seen as a terrifying adversary, it's important to recognize that the emu holds a place of reverence and respect among Aboriginal peoples across Australia. The Wiradjuri people, among others, see emus as creator spirits. These majestic birds play a crucial role in the Dreamtime stories that map the spiritual and earthly worlds.

The Emu in the Sky constellation, unlike the more defined constellations crafted by stars, is a dark constellation. It is traced not by the light of stars but by the dark spaces in the Milky Way, which creates the silhouette of an emu stretching across the night sky. This constellation is visible in the Southern Hemisphere's autumn and winter skies.

As the constellation rises in the sky, it signals the time for collecting emu eggs, a practice shared by many Aboriginal communities across Australia. Emu eggs are not only a valuable food source but also hold cultural and spiritual significance. One Dreamtime tale tells the story of how the egg became a symbol of light. It began when the emu named Dinewan argued with the dancing bird, Brolga. As the quarrel went on, Brolga became so angry that he snatched an egg from Dinewan's nest before launching it into the sky. The egg then landed on a heap of firewood and broke open. The yolk suddenly burst into flames, lighting up the entire world below. This act created the sun.

Chapter 5: Totemic Bonds: Animals and Ancestors

If you search what a totem is on the internet, it will most likely tell you that a totem is a natural object, animal, or phenomenon that serves as an emblem for a group of people. However, this explanation barely scratches the surface of totemic bonds among the Aboriginal Australians.

Totems are not arbitrary; they signify a person's or clan's connection to their ancestors, the land, and the Dreamtime. These connections are viewed as real and living, influencing daily life and social structures.

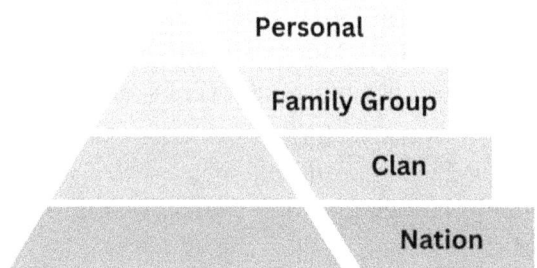

Totem structure in Aboriginal culture. (Created by author)

At the broadest level, the nation totem represents the collective spirit and identity of an Aboriginal nation. For example, the Wiradjuri Nation's totem is the gugaa, or the goanna. This creature embodies the qualities associated with the Wiradjuri people, such as resilience and strength. The nation totem links individuals to their wider community and the ancestral lands they inhabit.

Clan groups within these nations have their own totems, which act as identifiers and signify the unique characteristics or historical narratives of the clan. Strangers meeting for the first time can identify each other by their totems. Totems can signal who is likely to be friendly or not based on shared or complementary totemic affiliations and the intricate laws governing social interactions within and between different groups. This system has historically helped maintain peace and order and facilitated marriages and alliances of Aboriginal societies.

Another crucial aspect of this totemic identity is that it sort of determines who individuals can and cannot marry. In Aboriginal culture, people are not allowed to marry someone who shares the same totem as them. This is so that close relatives will not accidentally marry each other, preventing any health issues from appearing in future generations. This tradition also ensures diversity; people can create stronger bonds between different clans or family groups.

The personal totem is chosen by elders to reflect and honor the distinct qualities, strengths, and potential of a person. Unlike the inherited totems (the nation, clan, and family totems), the personal totem is assigned based on the individual's character, talents, life journey, or even weaknesses. This assignment is not bound by a specific timeline; it can occur at any stage of life. A child whose identity and inherent gifts are clear might receive their totem early on, allowing it to serve as a guide and protector through their formative years. For others, their personal totem might not be revealed until later in life. This flexibility ensures that the totem truly resonates with the individual's personal journey and growth.

The concept of moiety further deepens the totemic system's complexity. Moieties divide communities into two complementary halves, with each individual belonging to one moiety or the other. This division extends to totems.

For example, one moiety might have the gray kangaroo as a totem, while the other has the red kangaroo. Members of the gray kangaroo moiety are tasked with conserving and protecting the animal. The red kangaroo moiety might have permission to hunt and use the gray kangaroo but only within sustainable and sacred boundaries. This reciprocal arrangement ensures the survival of both species.

Of course, one of the cardinal rules within this system is that an individual is not allowed to harm or kill their own totem. This prohibition is rooted in the belief that the totemic animal or object is an ancestor, kin, or spiritual guardian. Harming it would be akin to harming one's own family or oneself.

Such responsibilities extend beyond mere protection or use. For example, the "emu people" are not only responsible for safeguarding emus but are also custodians of knowledge regarding their breeding cycles, habitats, and behaviors. This custodianship means that should an emu nest be raided or the birds' reproduction cycle be disturbed, the emu people are held accountable. They are expected to educate others, enforce protective measures, and rectify any harm to their totemic animal.

The totemic system acknowledges that while humans have needs that may involve using natural resources, they also have the duty to conserve, protect, and pass on a healthy and vibrant environment to future generations. Totems instill a sense of unity and interdependence that is central to Aboriginal cultures.

Examples of Totemic Animals

Totemic Animal	Region	Aboriginal Group(s)
Kangaroo	Various, widespread across Australia	Wiradjuri (New South Wales), Pitjantjatjara (Central Desert)
Emu	Various, widespread across Australia	Wiradjuri (New South Wales), Wotjobaluk (Victoria)
Crocodile	Northern Australia (Northern Territory, Queensland)	Yolngu (Arnhem Land), Gagudju (Kakadu National Park)
Wedge-tailed Eagle	Victoria	Kulin nation, Wurundjeri

Totemic Animal	Region	Aboriginal Group(s)
Turtle	Northern coastal areas (Queensland, Torres Strait)	Torres Strait Islanders, Coastal Queensland groups
Dolphin	Coastal regions, especially in Western Australia	Noongar (Southwestern Australia)
Brolga	Northern and northeastern Australia	Guugu Yimithirr (North Queensland)

Dreamtime Stories of the Kangaroo

The kangaroo is one of the most iconic creatures in Australia and holds immense cultural significance for Aboriginal Australians. The Arrernte people of Central Australia, for instance, revere the red kangaroo, which they refer to as kere aherre. Similarly, the Palawa people from Flinders Island, Tasmania, have the kangaroo as their totem. Despite the geographical distance and environmental differences from the mainland, the kangaroo is still an important symbol for the Palawa people.

Red kangaroos at Sturt National Park.[84]

Interestingly, the name "kangaroo" has its origins in the language of the Guugu Yimithirr people of far north Queensland. The word *gangurru* refers to a specific type of kangaroo and was first recorded by James Cook and his crew during their exploration of the region.

The animal's significance is not only due to the kangaroo's prominence in the Australian landscape but also because of its vital role in Indigenous cultures. For Aboriginal Australians, kangaroos have always been integral to their way of life, serving as a crucial source of food and playing a part in rituals, Dreamtime stories, and oral traditions.

The Dreamtime story of Bohra the kangaroo is a great example of the relationship between Aboriginal people and the kangaroo. There once was a time when an impenetrable darkness shrouded the world each night, making it impossible for the bright moon and stars to shine. During this time, a creature named Bohra roamed the land on all fours. Although he was adept at navigating the dim world, especially when he fed at night, he longed to see the world bathed in the gentle glow of the moon and stars. Instead of sitting by and hoping something would change, Bohra chose to take action.

As a wirinun, or a magician of great power, Bohra rolled the darkness away, as if it was a rug covering the night sky. This allowed the moon and stars to light up the heavens, enabling him and other creatures to see clearly during the night.

Later, Bohra found himself drawn to the sight of fire and the melody of distant singing. His curiosity led him to a sacred gathering—a corroboree of tribespeople moving rhythmically around a fire. Moved by an irresistible urge, Bohra stepped into the light, tentatively rising onto his hind legs in an attempt to join the dance.

The tribespeople were taken aback by the sight, but at the same time, they were enthralled by Bohra's presence. He continued to dance awkwardly, trying to mimic their movements. However, as a consequence of intruding on the sacred corroboree uninvited, the tribal wirinun declared that Bohra must be punished. Since he had shown the tribe a new dance, the punishment of death was ruled out. Instead, Bohra and his descendants would be bound to move by jumping on their hind legs, using their forefeet as hands and their tails for balance. This curse also granted Bohra a place within the tribe, signifying the kangaroo's enduring bond with Aboriginal people.

Bohra's canine teeth were knocked out as part of his initiation into the tribe. The men of the tribe fashioned false tails, adorning themselves to mimic their new kin. The kangaroo dance, born from that night, became an integral part of their sacred rituals.

Another Dreamtime tale tells of how the kangaroo got its tail. There once lived two friends: Mirram the kangaroo and Warreen the wombat. In those days, both Mirram and Warreen were men, and they walked the land in harmony.

Warreen had a knack for craftsmanship, and he constructed a lovely humpy or gunyah for himself. This small, temporary shelter, woven from soft bark and lined with leaves, offered him a cozy refuge. Mirram, on the other hand, found comfort in the soft grass beneath him, which served as his mattress, and the star-studded sky above, which he considered his quilt. The thought of a shelter never crossed his mind.

That was until the skies opened up one day, unleashing a heavy downpour that Mirram had never seen before. Mirram was soaked to the bone and, shivering, sought refuge in Warreen's gunyah. Warreen refused to let Mirram enter. Left out in the cold, Mirram's frustration brewed into a storm fiercer than the one raging around him.

Mirram conceived a dark plan. He dragged an enormous rock to the entrance of Warreen's shelter. Mirram smashed the rock upon Warreen's unsuspecting head. The impact startled Warreen and flattened his head. However, by some miracle, his life was spared.

"Oh, you wicked Mirram. How could you hurt your dearest friend?" Warreen asked.

"A friend? You are mean and selfish, Warreen!" Mirram angrily responded.

A wombat in Narawntapu National Park, Tasmania.[85]

Warreen's thoughts turned to vengeance. He bided his time until an opportunity presented itself. One day, Mirram was chasing a possum. Warreen lifted a spear and stealthily approached Mirram. With a swift thrust, he pierced Mirram's back, embedding the spear so deeply that it became a part of him, transforming into a long, spear-like tail.

From that day forward, Mirram thumped the ground with his tail with every leap, a constant reminder of Warreen's revenge. He never again sought shelter. Warreen bore the mark of the rock's blow, and his descendants were forever distinguished by their flat heads, serving as a lesson for selfishness and the cost of revenge.

Wayamba the Turtle

The Arakwal people of Byron Bay, nestled in a picturesque coastal region, have long been guardians of the land and sea that define their home. Among the many totems revered by the Arakwal people is the turtle, or Binguing as they call it. Because of the Binguing, the Arakwal people know how to live in harmony with the marine environment, ensuring its protection for future generations. Even to this day, surfers and swimmers can often catch a glimpse of turtles swimming to the surface of the bay for air.

Byron Bay.[56]

"The turtle is a free spirit and can glide gracefully through the ocean for over a hundred years. Many people can see the joy in the spirit of a turtle because it lives as though it doesn't have a worry in the world."

-Luke Mallie, an artist of both Aboriginal and Torres Strait Island descent[34]

The Dreamtime tells the story of the first turtle. The story of Wayamba begins with Oola the lizard, who was out gathering yams on the Mirrieh flat with her three children. There was no danger in sight, and the mother and children took their time. However, their foraging was soon interrupted by the rustling of something large in the bushes. Oola squinted her eyes, trying to get a better look at what lurked in there. Suddenly, Wayamba burst forth, startling Oola and her three children.

Wayamba had no intention to harm them. He actually expressed his desire to take Oola as his wife. He even offered to bring her children to his camp. Oola was intimidated by Wayamba's spear and boondi (a type of hardwood club), so she reluctantly agreed to follow him to his camp.

However, upon their arrival, Wayamba's tribe expressed their discontent. They were furious that Wayamba had brought Oola and her children without seeking the approval of her tribe. They warned Wayamba of the inevitable conflict with Oola's tribe, as they would surely come to reclaim her.

"We shall not help you if they come," Wayamba's chief told him. "Now, you must go to the plains and do your own fighting."

As predicted, Oola's tribe soon arrived, their bodies covered in war paint and their weapons at the ready. Wayamba He armed himself with two large shields, one covering his front and the other slung against his back. He then took up his weapons. As he stepped onto the plains, the air was pierced by the sound of sharp spears and boomerangs launched by Oola's tribe. Wayamba drew his limbs inside the shields and ducked his head, miraculously surviving the onslaught.

The spears fell to the ground, but the attackers had no plans to give up. They closed in, forcing Wayamba to retreat toward a creek. Cornered and with no ground left to give, Wayamba discarded his front shield and leaped into the creek. Oola's tribe waited, their spears poised to strike should Wayamba resurface. However, their wait was in vain. Wayamba was never seen again.

---

[34] *Dreamtime Stories: The Turtle.* (2020, August 13). Yarn Marketplace. https://www.yarn.com.au/blogs/yarn-in-the-community/dreamtime-stories-the-turtle
Dreamtime Story: The Seven Sisters. (2020, December 8). Yarn Marketplace.

Instead, in the waterhole where Wayamba had vanished, they encountered a peculiar creature they had never seen before. This being had a fixed plate on its back like a shield and could draw in its head and limbs when threatened. This marked the birth of the first turtle.

A hawksbill sea turtle, a critically endangered species.[87]

The Crow, an Animal of Tricks and Cunning

In another story of the Aboriginal people, particularly within the Kulin nation of central Victoria, the crow holds a place of great importance. Known in their tongue as Waa or Waang, the crow is regarded as one of their two moieties or ancestral spirits, with the other being the eagle-hawk Bunjil.

An Australian raven.[88]

One such legend told orally by the Wurundjeri people of the Kulin nation talks about the origin of fire, a gift that forever changed the lives of all beings. The secret of fire was guarded by the seven Karatgurk sisters who called the banks of the Yarra River (the location of urban Melbourne) their home. These women carried live coals on the ends of their digging sticks, which they used to ignite flames for cooking murnong yams, a staple in their diet.

One day, the crow stumbled upon a cooked yam lying on the ground. Upon tasting it, he was struck by the realization that cooked food was far superior to the raw fare he was accustomed to. This ignited a desire within him to cook his own food. He approached the Karatgurk sisters and asked them to share their fire. However, they refused; they were protective of the power they wielded.

Not one to be easily deterred, the crow devised a clever plan to obtain fire. He first caught several snakes before concealing them within an ant mound. Then, he invited the women over and told them he had just tasted ant larvae. He claimed they were exceptionally delicious, even more so than the cooked yam. Believing the cunning crow, the women decided to try the larvae. As they began to dig into the mound, they disturbed the snakes concealed in it. Angry, the snakes attacked the women, who let out loud shrieks. They began hitting the snakes with their digging sticks as hard as they could. In the ensuing chaos, the live coals were dislodged from their digging sticks. The crow swiftly collected the coals, stowing them away in a kangaroo skin bag.

When the Karatgurk sisters realized they had been tricked, they pursued the crow, who eluded capture by taking to the skies. From his perch high atop a tree, the crow watched his pursuers' efforts.

The commotion attracted Bunjil the eagle-hawk. He was intrigued by the crow's discovery of fire and requested some coals to cook a possum. Instead of handing one to the eagle-hawk, the crow offered to cook the possum. Word of the crow's possession of fire spread, leading others to demand he share this precious knowledge. In a moment of panic, the crow flung live coals to the crowd, and the fire-tailed finch, Kurok-goru, caught some. The finch tucked them behind his back, which is the reason why firefinches have red tails to this day. Bunjil's shaman helpers, Djurt-djurt the nankeen kestrel and Thara the quail hawk, also helped gather the rest of the coals.

A wedge-tailed eagle, a species that Bunjil is often depicted as.[89]

However, the scattered coals led to a bushfire, scorching the crow's feathers black. The fire threatened to engulf the land until Bunjil intervened. The Karatgurk sisters were swept into the heavens, turning into the Pleiades. Their glowing fire sticks shine down as stars and act as a celestial reminder of how fire came to people.

Chapter 6: Boomerangs: More Than Just a Piece of Wood

When speaking of Australia, some may immediately think of the boomerang, a piece of exquisitely crafted wood that flies back to the thrower. Known worldwide and often brought home by tourists as souvenirs, it is often seen as a cultural novelty. However, boomerangs actually hold a far deeper significance that goes beyond what meets the eye.

The Aborigines never thought of the boomerang as only a simple tool. Every inch of it contains a story. Its unique, circular flights, for instance, are thought to mirror the cycle of life, death, and rebirth; this is a central concept to Aboriginal spirituality where all things are interconnected.

Boomerangs come in various shapes and designs, and they are crafted with a specific purpose and cultural meanings. The most popular one is the returning boomerang. Known for its ability to fly in a curved path and return to the thrower, this type of boomerang is designed specifically for precision and control. Typically lighter, this type of boomerang often has a distinctive twist in its wings. This specific design allows them to catch the air and complete a full loop.

There are non-returning boomerangs. Designed for straightforward power, this type of boomerang flies in a direct line rather than returning back to the thrower. In contrast to the returning boomerang, this particular boomerang is usually larger and weighs significantly more. With its symmetrical shape, a non-returning boomerang can maintain a straight, forceful path.

The cross boomerang serves a whole different function. With four equal arms extending from a central point, cross boomerangs are usually used for ceremonial purposes such as dances, storytelling, and rituals rather than hunting. They are often made from wood or metal and sport a hole in the center.

Since boomerangs hold a deeper significance to the Aboriginal Australians, it is not surprising when people put extra care into crafting one. The process starts with selecting the right wood. This is perhaps the most critical step. The choice of wood used can affect the boomerang's shape, weight, and, of course, durability. Mulga wood is known to be rather dense and strong, making it the perfect wood for boomerangs used for hunting. In contrast, she-oak is lighter and easier to carve out intricate designs. Boomerangs made from this wood are more suited for ceremonial purposes.

Regardless of the wood choice, it is also important to ensure that the wood is dry and free of knots and cracks. To ensure that the wood is suitable for shaping, the makers prefer to harvest wood straight from the branches or roots, which naturally have slight bends. However, there are some who prefer to use driftwood or fallen logs.

After choosing the right wood, the shaping process begins. To strip the wood down to a rough outline, the makers use an array of tools such as stone axes, knives, or controlled fire. The shape itself varies on the intended use. If someone is crafting a boomerang for hunting, the maker would shape it to be longer and straighter, making precision and impact the main attributes of the boomerang. Those intended for ceremonial use, however, are often fashioned with more unique curves or additional bends, making them appear more distinctive than the ones used for hunting.

Once the boomerangs are shaped, it is then time for them to be smoothed and polished. Makers utilize sandpaper, emery, or even animal skins to remove the rough edges and reduce imperfections. The ultimate goal is to refine the boomerang's surface so that it can slice through the air smoothly. It is only after achieving the right level of smoothness that the makers move on to the next step: decoration. This is where intricate carvings and paintings of animals, plants, and landscapes or tribe symbols are made to embellish the look of the boomerangs.

Of course, these decorations are not only for design; each of these cultural expressions carries a unique meaning. Boomerangs with an image of a kangaroo, for example, are thought to symbolize agility and resilience, while a snake embodies wisdom and transformation. As for the coloring process, the makers always make sure to use colors that are derived from natural sources, such as ochre, charcoal, clay, or plant juices. These colors are applied with either brushes, sticks, or fingers. Once the coloring process is done, the boomerang is covered in a protective layer of resin, wax, or oil so that it can withstand both Mother Nature and the passage of time.

Last but not least, the boomerang must be tuned. Its angles, balance, and aerodynamics are put to the test, ensuring that it can fly in the way it should. If needed, makers will bend or twist the wood, shave down certain parts of the boomerang, or add subtle weights to achieve the desired flight pattern. This is a process of trial and error; the makers will test and refine the boomerang until it meets their standards.

The Origins of Boomerang According to Dreamtime Stories

This Dreamtime story begins with the Rainbow Serpent resting on a hill. Under the sunlight, its scales glinted so shimmery that it caught the attention of a group of hunters. Enthralled by the beauty of the serpent's multicolored scales and consumed by greed, the hunters felt the desire to take the scales for themselves.

"There is only one way to do this," one of the greedy hunters said. "We have to kill the Rainbow Serpent."

Eager to get their hands on the beautiful scales, the hunters made their move. Slowly, they readied their spears and crouched closer to the resting serpent. With a fixed aim, they hurled their spears at the magnificent creature. However, their spears were no match for the mighty Rainbow Serpent, as its scales were extremely tough, perhaps imbued with magic and divine powers. The spears bounced off its scales, and surprisingly, they flew back toward the hunters. Seeing this, the greedy hunters immediately fled in terror; they realized they had underestimated the mighty power of the Rainbow Serpent.

This, however, is not the end of the story. Angered, the Rainbow Serpent eventually decided to teach the greedy hunters a lesson. The serpent uncurled its great body, plucked one of its own glinting scales, and hurled it after the hunters. This magical scale flew through the air in a wide curve and struck one of the hunters in the back. With fear completely overtaking them, the hunters fled for good. Knowing that the lesson had been delivered, the serpent was able to enjoy its peace once again.

As the great serpent was about to return to its rest, it saw one remaining hunter nearby. Unlike the others, this hunter had been the only one who had refrained from attacking the Rainbow Serpent earlier. So, the Rainbow Serpent rewarded him. The great spirit offered the wise hunter one of its shimmering scales and gave detailed instructions on how he could use it. This scale became the very first boomerang, serving as a tool of sustenance and survival for the Aboriginal people for countless generations.

The Binbinga people of northern Australia have told their own story that explains the origin of the boomerang. It also involves a giant serpent, which they refer to as Bobbi-Bobbi; its difference from the Rainbow Serpent is that Bobbi-Bobbi lived in the heavens, watching over the earth below. Bobbi-Bobbi was thought to be a gentle and benevolent spirit who never failed to help humans thrive.

The serpent, gazing down from the skies, noticed the humans' struggle. Despite having shelter and enough water, they were struggling to find enough food. So, Bobbi-Bobbi, always known for his compassion, decided to lend a hand. Using his magical powers, the giant serpent created flying foxes—a species of large bats native to Australia—so that the people could hunt them for meat and nourishment.

This did not solve the problem, as the bats soon flew too high for the humans to catch. Determined to see humans prosper, Bobbi-Bobbi came up with another creation. The giant serpent shaped one of his own ribs into the world's first-ever boomerang. He then handed down his new creation to the humans and taught them to throw it at the flying foxes. For this, the humans were grateful; they no longer had to battle with hunger every day.

However, humans could never escape their own greed. Despite being grateful for the gift, some wanted more. Two men, in particular, became curious and wished to see the heavens where Bobbi-Bobbi dwelled. They hatched a plan, and when others asked them about their intentions, the two pretended they wanted to thank the giant serpent in person. The two men threw the boomerang into the sky, slicing through the clouds and creating a hole in the celestial realm. This action startled Bobbi-Bobbi to the point he failed to catch the boomerang in time. It fell back to the earth, striking the two men who had thrown it. They were killed, marking the first time death ever confronted humans.

As for Bobbi-Bobbi, the giant serpent was terribly saddened by their reckless act. He retreated further into the heavens, never again interfering in human affairs.

The Eagle and the Crocodile: The Creators of the Boomerang

Another story that explains the origin of the boomerang centers around the Eagle. Held in high regard in many Dreamtime stories, especially for its strength and keen intelligence, the Eagle was also thought to be the ruler of the skies, watching over the lives of the creatures that dwelled below. One day, the Eagle spotted a group of kangaroos grazing peacefully. Hungry, the Eagle decided to capture one of them for a hearty meal.

The kangaroos, ever alert, quickly evaded capture the moment they saw the Eagle swooping down from the sky. Although frustrated, the Eagle was not one to give up; it attempted to capture one of the kangaroos again, only for the kangaroo to successfully dodge its sharp talons. At this point, the Eagle knew it had to be creative, as its usual hunting tactics were not working. After a moment of thinking, the Eagle flew to a nearby tree, where it snapped off a branch. With patience and precision, the Eagle shaped and molded the wood until it turned into a curved stick—a boomerang.

With this new tool, the Eagle returned to the skies and looked for the kangaroos. Once it spotted them, the Eagle threw the curved stick at them. The boomerang spun through the air in a wide arc. Finally, one of the kangaroos fell victim to this tool, stunning it long enough for the Eagle to swoop down and claim its long-awaited meal. Satisfied with its creation, the Eagle soon felt the need to share this new knowledge. It gathered other birds and taught them how to craft and use the boomerang.

While this story revolves around a hungry Eagle, there is another tale that speaks of the boomerang's origin. Almost similar to the tale of the Eagle, the Crocodile's story begins with the animal feeling a tinge of hunger as it rested in a river. Noticing a school of fish swimming near the surface, the Crocodile made a move; it snapped its powerful jaws, hoping it could catch at least one. However, these fish were too fast, and they darted away before the Crocodile's teeth could close around them.

The Crocodile tried again, yet he was met with only frustration. The fish were too slippery and swift. The Crocodile went away and swam to the riverbank. Upon stumbling upon a strong root growing nearby, the Crocodile began to think of an idea. After digging the root out, the Crocodile let natural instinct guide its creation. He eventually shaped the root into a curved blade using only his sharp teeth and claws.

The Crocodile quickly swam back toward the location where the fish were swimming. It hurled the curved blade at the water, and the boomerang spun in a slicing motion, cutting through one of the fish with ease. The Crocodile was impressed by his new creation, and he chose to share it with the other reptiles so that they could catch their prey more effectively.

Wurruna, the Young Hunter Who Ended Drought

There was a time when the earth was nothing but dry and barren. A skilled young hunter named Wurruna planned to save his people. Not only were rivers and ponds a thing of the past, but the once-abundant land now lay parched beneath the merciless sun, leaving his tribe starving. Wurruna knew it was only a matter of time before his people would succumb to the worst fate of all. Armed with his spear and club and accompanied by his two loyal dogs, the young hunter embarked on a journey to restore hope back to his land.

For a long time, he traveled across the vast plains and rugged hills, where he encountered an array of strange and wonderful creatures. He saw the prickly echidna scurrying across the dust, the elegant emu standing proud, and the kangaroo using its powerful hind legs to leap through the air.

Apart from animals, Wurruna also encountered an old man during his journey. The elder was said to have sensed the weariness in Wurruna's eyes, and he offered the hunter a gift: a magic stone that could produce water wherever it was thrown. Wurruna was overjoyed with the gift. He expressed his gratitude to the old man before placing the stone safely in his pack and continuing his journey.

Days later, the young hunter's perseverance finally paid off when he stumbled upon a lake brimming with fish. Wurruna set up his camp by the lake. Making use of his hunting skills, he cast his spear into the water, successfully catching several fish for a meal. He cooked them over a small fire and savored them. Suddenly, a creature appeared, flying above the lake in lazy circles. Wurruna concluded that it was none other than a brolga (a species of bird native to southeastern Australia and New

Guinea). Captivated by the bird's beauty, Wurruna planned to catch the brolga and turn it into his pet.

The young hunter aimed his spear, and after a deep breath, he hurled it toward the brolga. However, Wurruna had underestimated the bird, as it easily dodged it. The brolga then let out a playful call, as if trying to mock Wurruna for missing. Not one to back down, Wurruna reached for his club and threw it at the mocking brolga. Again, the hunter missed. Interestingly, the club did not fall to the ground. Instead, it spun in a loop and made its way back into Wurruna's hand. Amazed by this new weapon, Wurruna named this creation the boomerang after the whirling sound it made as it spun through the air.

His excitement for this new weapon did not divert his attention away from the brolga. He threw his boomerang in the direction of the bird again and again but failed to bring the brolga down each time. The bird flew higher in the sky and taunted the young hunter even more. Wurruna chased after the bird and threw his boomerang again and again. But while doing so, he accidentally left a trail of water across the land. It turned out that his magic stone had slipped from his bag onto the boomerang. Each time he threw the boomerang, a small stream of water poured from the stone. This created rivers, lakes, and ponds across the landscape, transforming the barren earth into a planet full of life.

The cat-and-mouse chase went on between Wurruna and the brolga. The young hunter eventually managed to corner the bird at the edge of a steep cliff, where he threw the boomerang one last time. The brolga caught the boomerang mid-air with its beak and flew off into the sky. Wurruna could do nothing except watch the bird fly away with his new invention—and the magic stone with it. The young hunter was heartbroken. He fell to his knees, feeling as though he had lost everything.

The brolga, on the other hand, spotted a group of people who appeared to be celebrating something. The bird landed and found out that these people were from Wurruna's tribe; they had been following the trail of water that Wurruna had unknowingly left behind. When they found the newly formed waterhole nearby, the people gathered around to rejoice at the bounty that had returned to their land. Perhaps affected by their joy, the brolga decided to join in the celebration, dropping the boomerang and dancing around with the humans. The tribe welcomed the bird with open arms.

The boomerang, which had been left on the ground, was eventually found by Wurruna's loyal dogs. Recognizing that it was their master's previous invention, the dogs picked it up with their mouths. The magic stone was nowhere to be found, though. The dogs hurried back to the cliff where Wurruna remained in despair. The sight of his dogs carrying his boomerang filled the young hunter's heart with both gratitude and relief. He hugged his companions, thanking them for their loyalty.

As he stood and looked down the cliff, getting ready to move on with his journey, Wurruna noticed his tribe dancing and celebrating by the waterhole. He was surprised at first, but joy immediately took over as he realized that his journey had not been in vain after all. Although he had lost his magic stone and failed to capture the brolga, Wurruna had successfully brought back life to the land. Not only that, the young hunter had also created a tool that would benefit his people for generations to come. Perhaps embracing the wisdom of the journey, Wurruna chose to forgive the brolga for its mocking.

Upon joining his tribe in their celebration, Wurruna took the chance to show his people the boomerang, teaching them how to use the tool. The boomerang became a cherished part of their lives, and Wurruna was hailed as a hero.

Chapter 7: Ethics and Morality in Aboriginal Legends

Throughout the history of human civilization, myths have served as a foundational pillar. From the ancient Greeks to the Egyptians and the Norse, each culture has harnessed the power of myths to convey important lessons.

In Greek mythology, tales of Icarus, who flew too close to the sun, and Prometheus, who stole fire for humanity resulting in Zeus's wrath, underscore the dangers of overreaching one's ambition and the value of restraint. Egyptian myths emphasized the balance of Ma'at, or order, over Isfet, chaos.

Aboriginal myths and legends also imparted wisdom and ethical guidelines. Through these stories, knowledge, cultural values, and laws are transmitted from one generation to the next, ensuring the survival of Aboriginal heritage and wisdom.

Tiddalik the Frog

Back when the earth was very young, there lived a creature named Tiddalik the frog. Tiddalik was not an ordinary frog. He was small, mischievous, and greedy. One day, the glow of the sun woke Tiddalik from his short nap.

Tiddalik awoke with a thirst unlike any he had felt before. Driven by this insatiable desire, Tiddalik began to drink. He drank from the billabongs, their waters cool and refreshing. He drank from the rivers, where the fish darted in silver flashes beneath the surface. He drank from the streams, their babbling voices quieted by his endless thirst.

As Tiddalik drank, he grew bigger and bigger. However, the world around him began to change too. The billabongs shrank, their muddy beds exposed to the scorching sun. The rivers slowed, their currents weakened, and the streams whispered no more. The land became parched, and the trees drooped. The animals gathered in the dwindling shade, confused. As Tiddalik drank, the water in the world began to disappear.

Soon, the creatures of the land came together to voice their concerns. They knew that if Tiddalik's thirst was not quenched, the world would be devoid of water. A wise wombat came up with a plan. They would make Tiddalik laugh; if he laughed, the water he had consumed would surely be released, returning to the world.

The animals decided to host a corroboree, where they began their attempts to entertain Tiddalik. The first to come forth was the kangaroo. He danced, his legs kicking up dust in a comical display. Yet, Tiddalik did not even crack a smile. Next, it was the lizard's turn. He waddled on his two legs, making his stomach stick out. The other animals laughed at his silly act, but Tiddalik remained unfazed.

"Surely a little joke or a funny story would make him laugh," said the kookaburra. However, the kookaburra also failed to entertain Tiddalik.

A kookaburra, a bird native to Australia, known for its laughing call.[40]

Hope was beginning to disappear until the arrival of Nabanum the eel. Nabanum danced in front of Tiddalik. His body contorted into outlandish shapes. He danced and danced, his speed increasing until he accidentally entangled himself into a knot. There was a moment of silence. Tiddalik could not contain himself. A chuckle bubbled up from his huge belly. He then let out a burst of laughter that shook the leaves from the trees and ruffled the feathers of the birds.

As he laughed, the waters he had consumed burst forth in a great deluge. This filled the rivers, streams, and billabong. The animals sighed in relief.

Tiddalik returned to his initial form. He realized that it was not nice to be greedy and that sharing will always make the world a better place. Tiddalik reminded himself to take only what he needs when he needs it.

The story of Tiddalik teaches that personal needs and desires must be balanced with the well-being of others, a lesson of moderation and communal responsibility that is as relevant today as it was in the Dreamtime.

Though versions of this story are found in many Aboriginal cultures, it is often attributed to the Gunaikurnai people of South Gippsland, Victoria. The story of Tiddalik is thought to have been inspired by the behavior of the water-holding frog (*Ranoidea platycephala*), an amphibian native to central Australia. These frogs have developed an extraordinary adaptation to their arid environment. They burrow underground during dry periods, emerging with the rains to absorb significant amounts of water. This unique behavior allows them to breed, feed, and, most importantly, avoid drying out during times of drought. In times of scarcity, Indigenous Australians would gently squeeze these frogs to obtain water.

The *Ranoidea platycephala*, commonly known as the water-holding frog.[a]

However, the original tale, as recounted by some Aboriginal groups, ends with a rather somber reflection on the consequences of Tiddalik's actions. In this older version, the flood resulting from Tiddalik's laughter does not just replenish the world; it also brings about an environmental catastrophe. The flood causes widespread drowning, with many animals losing their lives and others finding themselves stranded on newly formed islands. Borun the pelican came to the aid of those stranded, ferrying them to safety.

The story of Tiddalik, in all its variations, teaches us about the importance of living in harmony with nature, the dangers of greed, and the responsibility we have to protect and preserve the world for future generations.

Another Aboriginal story that centers around the theme of greed involves the intriguing tale of two brothers-in-law, Gandji and Wurrpan. One warm day, Gandji, accompanied by his children, ventured to the water to spearfish for stingrays. With skill honed by years and patience, they speared several stingrays. The catch of the day was bountiful, and with spirits high, they set about preparing their feast.

They cleaned and filleted the fish. They gathered firewood to cook their catch, the air heavy with the scent of the sea mingled with the smell of smoke. The division of their spoils cast a shadow on their success. They wrapped the stingrays in bark, creating two portions—one filled with the succulent pieces and the other with the tougher parts.

Upon returning to their camp, Gandji presented Wurrpan's family with the lesser portion, keeping the more delectable share for himself and his children. Wurrpan and his family immediately noted the poor texture and taste. When Wurrpan learned of the unfair division, he confronted Gandji, arguing that fairness dictated the better pieces to be shared equally between their families.

Gandji was taken aback by the complaint and retorted, "If you desired the sweeter flesh, you should have taken to the waters yourself instead of awaiting our return." What started as a discussion soon escalated into an argument, with the two hurling insults at each other.

Neither side was willing to yield. In a fit of rage, Gandji grabbed a fistful of hot coals and a rock that he used for grinding nuts. He hurled them at Wurrpan, striking him squarely in the chest. Fearing that Wurrpan might retaliate, Gandji began to jump frantically, his leaps growing unnaturally high until he found himself soaring above the ground. As he ascended, his form began to morph. He grew feathers, and his body elongated into the shape of a bird—the jabiru—although he had no beak.

Wurrpan went to fetch his spear. Finding it too cumbersome, he shortened it before launching it skyward. His aim was precise. The spear pierced Gandji from the back of his head and through his face, making the protruding spear look like a beak. Gandji lost his balance, and he plummeted to the earth.

Wurrpan, with his children in tow, fled. As they ran, their bodies stretched into the slender, elegant forms of emus. Their feathers took on the gray hue of the ash from the coals, and a lump marked the spot where the smooth stone had struck Wurrpan. The unique shape of emu eggs mirrors the shape of the stone thrown by Gandji.

Lungkata the Blue-Tongued Lizard Who Lied

A blotched blue-tongued lizard, found in Tasmania, Australia.[48]

While the stories of Tiddalik and the skirmishes between Gandji and Wurrpan serve as moral lessons about greed and the consequences of selfishness, another tale from the heart of Australia emphasizes the importance of honesty.

Lungkata, a blue-tongued lizard man, traveled from the far north. He was drawn to Uluru because of its tales of beauty and community. He found a cozy cave that offered shelter and a splendid view of the sprawling landscape below.

One day, under the blazing sun, Panpanpalala, the crested bellbird man, was out hunting. With a well-aimed throw, he speared an emu. However, the emu, whose wings were too weak to fly, bolted toward

Uluru. The story sometimes whispers of Panpanpalala having a brother, making them a pair rather than a lone hunter. However, according to Jacob Puntaru, an Anagu elder, the most important thing about these stories is not the details but rather the lessons they teach.

Lungkata was also out searching for food. While he was on the hunt, his eyes fell upon the emu. It was wounded yet still breathing. He could see a spear lodged firmly in its side—a clear sign that it was already claimed by another hunter. Despite this, Lungkata decided to take the emu for himself, killing it with his stone ax. He then lit a fire and started to prepare his meal. However, not long after that, Lungkata heard the footsteps of an approaching stranger. It was Panpanpalala, who had been tracking his emu.

"Did you, by any chance, come across a wounded emu?" Panpanpalala asked.

Lungkata had managed to hide his stolen meal before Panpanpalala got close. He tried hard to conceal his panic.

"No, I haven't seen any emu," he answered.

Panpanpalala breathed a sigh of disappointment and left Lungkata alone. He had been tracking the emu for hours, yet there was no sight of it. But Panpanpalala eventually sniffed out Lungkata's deceit. He noticed the emu's tracks near where Lungkata had been camping.

Realizing the imminent return of Panpanpalala, Lungkata hastily gathered what he could of the emu meat and fled to the west. However, his escape was hasty, and he dropped a trail of pieces of the emu, including its thigh, which is still visible today at Kalaya Tjunta, just north of the Ikari cave near Mutitjulu Waterhole.

The path Lungkata left was glaringly obvious. It wasn't long before Panpanpalala caught up to him. Lungkata scrambled up Uluru, hoping he could escape from Panpanpalala and live another day. However, fate had another ending in store for the blue-tongued lizard. Under the watchful eyes of Uluru, Panpanpalala built a bonfire beneath Lungkata as the lizard struggled upward toward his cave.

The fire grew, eventually reaching Lungkata. Choked by smoke and licked by flames, Lungkata's desperate escape turned into a downfall. He tumbled down the face of Uluru, his body leaving a trail of scorched marks on the sacred rock. As he rolled, the heat stripped flesh from his body. Lungkata grew smaller, his form shrinking until all that was left of him was a single stone.

The Grim Tale of the Moonman

Before there was a moon to light the night sky, the Moonman walked the earth. He lived a simple life with his two wives and two sons. His wives were foragers, venturing into the bush to gather yams, berries, and plums, which sustained their family through the seasons.

As time passed, the two sons grew into teenagers. One day, filled with a burgeoning sense of responsibility and perhaps a dash of youthful arrogance, they approached their father with a declaration. They intended to go hunting. They wanted to provide for their family just as their father had always done. Moonman's heart swelled with pride at their words. He saw in them the reflection of his teachings and the promise of their growth into men of honor and skill.

And so, with their father's approval, the two sons set out to a big billabong. There, they showcased the skills their father had imparted to them, catching a variety of fish. A few hours later, their stomachs started grumbling, signaling that it was time for a hearty meal. They decided to cook a portion of their catch. Before long, a huge pile of fish sizzled over the fire, filling the air with tantalizing aromas.

Caught in the moment and seduced by their own greed, they feasted on the fish. With their hunger now satisfied, the two teenagers returned to their father bearing only the bony remnants of their selfish indulgence.

Moonman was delighted upon seeing his sons. However, his delight immediately dimmed when he discovered their haul was nothing but inedible bones. Stung by their father's disappointment yet unrepentant, the sons vowed to right their wrong. They promised a bounty of fish upon their next return. Yet, history repeated itself at the billabong. The lure of immediate satisfaction proved too strong, and once again, they indulged in the moment, leaving only bones to carry back to their father.

Moonman was outraged. He devised a devilish plan. First, he crafted a huge fishing trap out of kurrajong bark fiber. Once done, he handed it to his son.

"Let us use this trap when we go fishing another day," Moonman said to his sons.

The day eventually came. Moonman accompanied them to the billabong. He waited for the right moment, and as his sons lost themselves in the act of fishing, Moonman struck. Moonman used a big stick to beat his sons to death. He then left their bodies concealed within the very trap he had created and cast it into the billabong.

The next day, Moonman's wives returned from their foraging. They noticed the absence of their sons, so they immediately went to ask their husband. Unsurprisingly, Moonman chose to lie; he told his wives that their sons had gone fishing and that was the last time he had seen them. Upon learning this, the wives went to the billabong. There, they were confused by the water's crimson stain. They decided to pull the trap ashore and were struck by terror at what they found.

They cried for hours. Eventually, their grief morphed into anger. They carried the remains of their sons home. When the sky turned to night, the women set fire to their hut. Moonman was inside, deep asleep. He woke up seconds later, feeling as if he had been placed inside a blazing furnace.

Moonman screamed and made a desperate attempt to save himself. His escape led him to the top of a pandanus tree, where he declared his immortality.

"Remember this," Moonman shouted to his wives. "You'll disappear forever when you die. But I will come back immortal every month!"

In the heart of the Northern Territory is another tale of the moon's creation. This story centers around Japara, a man known far and wide for his exceptional skills as a hunter. Yet, this tale is really about hunting; rather, it is a story of love, loss, and redemption.

On a day like any other, while Japara was out providing for his family, a man named Parukapoli visited his home. Unlike Japara, whose prowess lay in tracking and spearing, Parukapoli's gift was in the art of storytelling. With a voice that could weave magic into words, Parukapoli told tales so captivating that Japara's wife became utterly entranced. She would become so absorbed in the stories that she would lose all sense of time and her duties. She did not even notice her baby son crawling away.

The baby's venture led him to a nearby stream, and he toppled into the water. Hearing the splash, Japara's wife rushed to save their son, but fate had already claimed the child.

When Japara returned and learned of the tragedy, his world crumbled. A fierce anger arose, and he blamed his wife for their loss. In a blind rage, he took up his hunting weapons and killed her. This act of violence was the spark that ignited a fierce confrontation with Parukapoli. The two fought each other, eventually resulting in Parukapoli's demise.

Left alone with his wounds and engulfed in a sea of grief, Japara faced the scorn of his tribe. They surrounded him, their voices raised not just in anger but also in disappointment. His actions had broken the sacred bonds of family and community.

"How could you kill your wife? She did not intend for any of this to happen!" they cried.

As the weight of his deeds settled upon his shoulders, Japara's heart began to open to the truth of his people's words. He returned to the location where he had left the bodies of his loved ones. Much to his sadness, the bodies were now gone; the spirits had taken them to a better place, a realm beyond his reach. Japara pleaded with the spirits, acknowledging his cruelty and expressing his yearning to be reunited with his family.

The spirits were moved by his remorse and granted him a path to the sky world, though not without conditions. As a penance for his actions, Japara was to wander the heavens, searching for his loved ones among the stars.

The moon that lights our night sky is said to be Japara's campfire, its glow a symbol of his eternal quest. The scars that mark the moon's surface remind us of Japara's earthly battles. Some say the moon waxes and wanes because Japara is forever changing camps. Others believe he has found them, and together, they explore the vast, mysterious expanse of the sky world.

This tale, like the moon's cyclical dance, speaks of the transformative power of love, the depths of despair, and the possibility of forgiveness. It reminds us that actions borne of anger can lead to irreversible consequences, but even in the darkest night, there is hope for redemption and reunion under the watchful eyes of our ancestors in the stars.

Chapter 8: Death, Rebirth, and the Afterlife

Back in the Dreamtime, a time when the world was young and the concept of death was unknown, the creatures of the earth lived in a state of perpetual existence. They never aged, and they never faded. Every morning brought the promise of infinity. However, this timeless tranquility was shattered one fine morning when a young cockatoo lost his grip while swinging high up in a tree. He fell, striking his head with such force that he lay still. The forest had never known such stillness.

The animals, bewildered by this unexpected turn of events, quickly gathered around. They attempted to wake the cockatoo from his peculiar slumber to no avail. The commotion soon drove the wise old wombat to see what could be done. He solemnly informed the others that their friend had broken his neck. The animals believed that this was the doing of the spirits. They had never witnessed their friends getting even the tiniest wound before, let alone death. The animals convened a meeting beneath a grand old gum tree to ponder this new dilemma.

During their discussion, the spirits lifted the little cockatoo into the sky, leaving the animals below to gaze in wonder as their friend ascended into the heavens.

"Worry not," the wise wombat said. "The spirits are doing no harm. They are merely transforming our friend into something new."

This notion sparked a mix of curiosity and hope among the animals. They asked each other who was brave enough to see if the wombat was speaking the truth. However, since winter had already blown its first cold breath, no one was eager to journey into the sky to witness the transformation—except for the caterpillars. The caterpillars ascended into the sky, hoping they could bear witness to the fate of their dear friend.

Days passed, and the animals, with the wise wombat leading the search, scoured the land for any sign of the caterpillars. They could find nothing. Then, on the first day of spring, the air was suddenly filled with a kaleidoscope of color. A parade of butterflies danced into view. The animals understood that the caterpillars had been reborn, transformed by the spirits into creatures of beauty and grace, just as their friend, the cockatoo, had been given a new form in the sky.

This transformation, the emergence of the butterfly from the cocoon, became a symbol of hope. This story tells us that change is an integral part of existence and a necessary part of life.

In Aboriginal culture, the journey through death and beyond is as deeply rooted in the community and the land as the journey through life. For the Aboriginal people, grieving is not merely an individual process. It is something that the whole community goes through together. They mourn not only to express sadness but also to embrace and celebrate the life and legacy of the person who has passed. This collective way of grieving undoubtedly helps to ease the pain.

Did you know?

> It is considered deeply inappropriate for individuals outside of the Worrorra, Ngarinyin, and Wunumbal tribes to paint or depict the Wandjina. These sacred spirits hold immense significance within these communities, and their portrayal is reserved exclusively for those in those tribes. Recognizing the importance of protecting this cultural heritage, the image of the Wandjina was trademarked in 2015 in an effort to prevent its misappropriation. Despite these measures, unauthorized use of the image of the Wandjina continues, highlighting the ongoing challenges in safeguarding Indigenous cultural expressions.

While at a glance, the Aboriginal response to death bears resemblances to European traditions—most notably in the ceremonial acknowledgment of death and the observance of mourning—such comparisons barely scratch the surface. While ceremonies and mourning are universal across cultures, Aboriginal spirituality infuses these practices with a profound connection to the land. For example, loved ones are often buried on ancestral land, and smoking ceremonies are sometimes performed to cleanse and guide the spirit back to the land. Death, as much as life, emphasizes the inseparable bond between the individual and the land. The deceased is seen not as departing from this connection but as entering into a new phase of existence. However, they will be forever entwined with the country of their birth.

Aboriginal beliefs hold that when a person dies, aspects of their spirit, along with their bones, return to the land where they were born. Thus, when someone passes away, the land feels the loss so deeply that trees may die or bear scars.

The transition from the physical world to the afterlife is a journey of the spirit back to the essence of creation or, rather, the womb of all time (Dreamtime). Life is a cycle with no true end. The concept of an afterlife in Aboriginal culture is different from Western notions of heaven and hell; it is not a place of reward or punishment but rather a return to the Land of the Dead, a realm that coexists with the living world.

The belief in the indestructibility of the human spirit is central to Aboriginal spirituality. Upon death, the spirit does not cease to exist; it transitions into the everywhen—a realm where time is non-linear and the spirit becomes one with the elements of nature.

Smoking Ceremonies

Smoking ceremonies hold a significant place in Aboriginal culture, especially in the mourning process. These ceremonies are performed at the location where the person passed away and within homes. They serve as a purification ritual and a means to guide the deceased's spirit peacefully to the afterlife. During these ceremonies, it's not uncommon for relatives to express their sorrow through physical manifestations of grief, such as cutting their hair or adorning their faces with white pigment.

Among the Western Arrernte people, it is believed that the soul travels to a distant island, integrating into the Dreamtime where ancestral spirits reside and continue to influence the world. In a similar vein, the Wandjina, revered figures in the Dreamtime stories of the Kimberley region, play a unique role in the transition to the afterlife. According to lore, upon choosing the place they would die, the Wandjina painted their images on cave walls. They then entered nearby waterholes, marking their passage from the physical world to the spiritual realm.

Other Central Australian Aboriginal groups envision the Land of the Dead as a celestial realm, a place among the stars where the spirits dwell. These diverse beliefs shape the funerary customs and ceremonies practiced by Aboriginal communities. Everyone wants to ensure the spirit's safe passage to the Land of the Dead.

Aboriginal cultures place great emphasis on the performance of specific rites and ceremonies, both in life and after death. These rites are seen as crucial for the spirit's transition, and it is believed that it is only through the completion of these rituals that the spirit can successfully navigate its way to the afterlife. The relatives of the deceased play a vital role in this process, carrying out postmortem ceremonies with great care and respect to honor the departed and aid their spirit on its journey. If people ignore this, then the spirit will not be able to move on, and it will resort to disturbing its living families.

Sorry Cuts

"Sorry cuts" are another form of expression of grief within some Aboriginal cultures. In the wake of a loss, individuals may make small cuts on their bodies, allowing the blood to flow as a physical release of their inner pain. This practice is deeply personal and is often surrounded by cultural taboos, including restrictions on discussing these acts of mourning with grieving family members.

Ceremonies and mourning periods are elaborate and can last for days, weeks, or even months. It is considered culturally inappropriate for a non-Aboriginal person to inform the next of kin of a person's passing, as this task is reserved for those within the cultural kinship system. This way, it ensures that the news is delivered with sensitivity and respect for traditional protocols.

The Aboriginal communities practice a concept called "sorry business," which encompasses the various practices associated with mourning and remembrance. This period of sorrow is not only a time for grieving but also a time for the community to heal, bringing together families to share in the loss, remember the deceased, and reaffirm the bonds that tie them to each other and to the land. During "sorry business," communities engage in storytelling, singing, and dancing, all of which serve to honor the deceased and facilitate their journey to the afterlife.

In many Aboriginal communities, burial rites are intricate. However, despite the variations, a common thread is the deep respect and care for the deceased, ensuring their safe passage to the afterlife and maintaining the harmony between the living, the land, and the spiritual world. Here are a few examples:

Burial Method	Description	Regions/Groups Known to Practice
Earth Burials	The body is placed in a grave dug into the ground, with variations in orientation and depth. Personal items may accompany the deceased.	Widespread across many Aboriginal cultures in Australia.
Platform Burials	Bodies are placed on raised platforms and left exposed to the elements. Bones may be collected, painted, and then buried or stored after decomposition.	Practiced in some communities, particularly in Arnhem Land (Northern Territory).
Tree Burials	The body is placed in the hollow of a tree, allowing for natural decomposition in a protected environment.	Known among certain groups, such as those in parts of Queensland.
Rock Shelter Burials	Bodies or bones are placed in rock shelters or caves, which protect the remains. These sites can be marked or decorated.	Common in regions with suitable geographical features, like the Kimberley (Western Australia).
Water Burials	The body is set adrift on a canoe or placed directly into water.	Less commonly documented but practiced by some coastal and islander communities.

Burial Method	Description	Regions/Groups Known to Practice
Secondary Burials	After initial decomposition, remains are collected for a second burial. It often involves rituals like painting bones with ochre and wrapping them for reburial.	Various Aboriginal cultures across Australia, with practices varying significantly between groups.

The Aboriginal practices of honoring those who have passed tell a story of life's unending rhythms. These traditions remind us that death is not simply an end but is also a passage—a bridge to something beyond our immediate grasp. This perspective shifts the weight of grief into a celebration of the natural cycle that connects all beings. It paints a picture of a world where the essence of those who have left us still lingers in the land they cherished, in the gentle rustling of trees, the soft murmur of streams, and the subtle whispers carried by the wind.

Chapter 9: Nature and Its Link to Aboriginal Myth

The Great Barrier Reef is a marvel of the natural world. It stretches over 2,300 kilometers (1,429 miles) along the northeastern coast of Australia. While many admire the beauty of the reef, for the Aboriginal people, particularly the Yidinji of the Gimoy (Cairns) region, it is a source of sustenance and a sacred site imbued with stories and spirits that trace back to the Dreamtime.

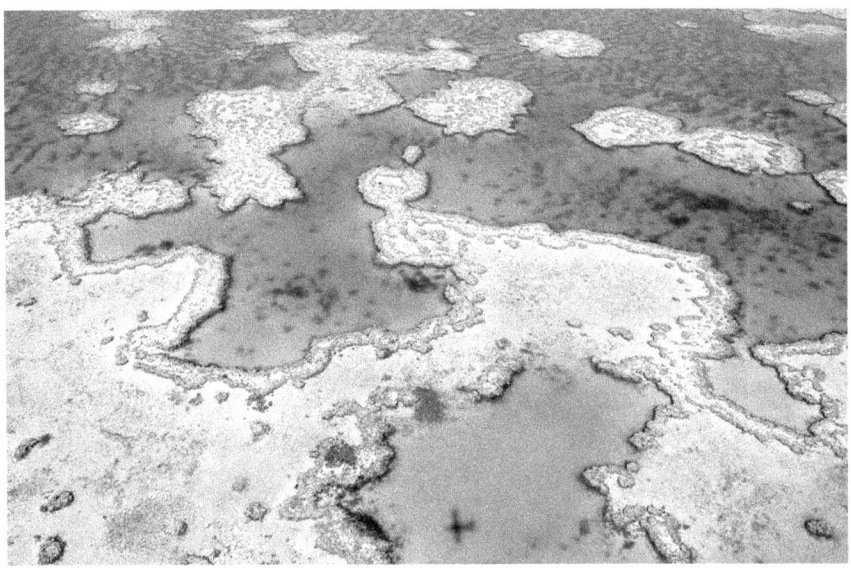

The Great Barrier Reef.[45]

One tale involving the Great Barrier Reef speaks of a time before the reef as we know it even existed. The story involves two brothers—others suggest a hunter and his two wives—whose actions brought them the wrath of their creator.

According to this tale, it all began with a creator named Bhiral placing a guardian fish in the sea where the Great Barrier Reef would soon form. This fish held such importance that it held the balance of the ecosystems in its fins. This particular fish was meant to keep harmony among the offshore islands. Bhiral, in his wisdom, had forbidden the spearing of this sacred creature; to harm it would be to unravel the very threads of life itself.

Yet, the brothers chose to defy the words of the mighty creator. They cast their spears into the water, striking the fish that was meant to remain unharmed. Their actions eventually reached Bhiral.

In his anger, Bhiral summoned the fire of the earth, hurling lava into the deep ocean. The sea boiled and rose. The brothers watched, their hearts sinking as the world around them changed. Where there was once only water, the cooling lava formed a new structure, a barrier that would stand as a reminder of their transgression. The Great Barrier Reef was born from their defiance.

These days, the Great Barrier Reef faces challenges that its ancient guardians could never have imagined. Marine scientist and coral specialist Charlie Veron—also known affectionately as the "Godfather of Coral"—has expressed profound sadness at the changes the reef has undergone. It has suffered from the impacts of climate change, pollution, and human activity. The corals, stressed by rising temperatures, have bleached, losing their colors and the life that once thrived among them.

The stories of the Yidinji and the teachings of elders and scientists highlight the urgent need to protect this precious ecosystem. In doing so, we honor not only the natural world but also the cultural heritage and wisdom that have been passed down through the generations.

Gulaga, the Mother Mountain

When Captain James Cook, the British explorer known for his voyages across the Pacific Ocean, first laid eyes on a majestic mountain along the southeastern coast of Australia, he named it Mount Dromedary due to its resemblance to a camel's hump. Little did he know, this particular mountain held a significance far beyond what he could have comprehended. To the Yuin people of southern New South Wales, this mountain, known as Gulaga, was and remains a sacred site.

Gulaga Mountain from Bermagui on the south coast of New South Wales. "

Did you know?

In the face of recurrent bushfires and drought, nearly one hundred Yuin nation individuals gathered at the foothills of Mount Gulaga in early December 2019. Coming from as far as Sydney and Victoria, they convened for a healing corroboree, a nationwide dance aimed at healing the country's spirit and land. Djiringanj elder Warren Ngarrae Foster highlighted the event's timeliness, noting, "Minga Gulaga had been crying. She has called her children back to come together at her feet to heal the spirit and country."

Gulaga is not just a mere mountain; she is Mother Mountain, a powerful symbol of motherhood, nurturing, and protection. To the Yuin, Gulaga represents the sacred birthplace—the spiritual origin of life and culture of the Yuin people. It is a crucial site for women's ceremonies, storytelling, and childbirth. Indigenous artist Cheryl Davison captures the essence of Gulaga, stating, "She's always been here. Gulaga is the Mother Mountain. Pregnant, she lies on her side, her head to the south, her feet to the north, facing the sea ... She was here when the stars and the moon and everything else was created ... she's always been here."[35]

---

[35] https://www.nma.gov.au/exhibitions/endeavour-voyage/gulaga-mount-dromedary.

The Dreamtime story of Gulaga and her two sons, Baranguba and Najanuga, speaks to the themes of adventure, protection, and the maternal bond. One day, as they were collecting bush tucker (also known as bush food, referring to any food native to Australia), Baranguba expressed his desire to go fishing. Gulaga advised against it, saying he was too young and that it was dangerous to venture alone. Despite her warnings, Baranguba's longing for independence and the call of the sea were too strong to resist.

In one version of the story, Baranguba sneaks away, crafts himself a canoe, and heads to the sea, only to be met by a formidable wave that washes him away. He is forced to lie in the ocean, transforming into an island that remains a part of the landscape to this day. Another telling of the tale sees Gulaga eventually relenting to her son's wishes, allowing him to venture into the ocean but not too far from her watchful gaze. Baranguba sets out, lying down in the ocean and turning into an island under the protective eye of his mother.

Witnessing his brother's departure, Najanuga also yearns for a space of his own. Yet, Gulaga asks him to stay close to her feet. Najanuga becomes a symbol of the child who stays by the mother, representing those who remain close to their roots and the protective embrace of the family. Today, the rock outcrop known as Najanuga or the Little Dromedary can be seen just to the east of Gulaga.

The Dreamtime Story of the Barramundi, Australia's Most Iconic Fish

Nestled in the heart of the East Kimberley region lies the Argyle Diamond Mine. This site is renowned worldwide for its deposits of pink and red diamonds. This mine transformed the landscape and brought the Western world's gaze to this remote part of Australia.

Long before the land was excavated for its precious stones, it was the setting for a Dreamtime story that explains the origin of the diamonds found there today. This tale tells of Daiwul, the giant barramundi.

To the Aboriginal people, the barramundi embodies the connection between the physical and spiritual worlds. This fish is an important part of Aboriginal people's dietary habits and is often represented in Aboriginal artworks that narrate the ancient stories and laws passed down through the generations. One such contemporary artwork by June Peters, an artist from Warmun, vividly brings to life the Barramundi Dreaming.

As the tale goes, Daiwul was no ordinary fish. She was colossal, and her skin shimmered with the promise of the Dreamtime. As she swam through the waters of Bow River, Daiwul caught the attention of three women. Perhaps enthralled by the barramundi, they decided to set out to catch Daiwul. In an attempt to get their hands on the shimmering fish, the women pushed down a wall of spinifex (a species of grass native to Australia) down the creek, hoping it could trap Daiwul. However, Daiwul leaped over the trap set by the women.

A barramundi.[45]

As Daiwul jumped over the hill behind Bow River, her underbelly scraped against the hill, causing a crack to form. The scales from her underbelly scattered across the countryside and became diamonds. Known as "rain stones" by the local Aboriginal people, they were believed to possess the power to summon rain when struck together and thrown into waterways.

At Gawinyin, or Cattle Creek Rockhole, the three women turned to stone, standing as eternal guardians at the water's edge. Visitors to the area can still witness these stone figures.

While Daiwul's tale narrates the origin of diamonds in the Kimberley region, another captivating dreamtime legend tells about the creation of the barramundi itself. This story tells of two young lovers bound by a love so immense that it defied the laws set by their tribe.

The lovers, whose union was forbidden under tribal law, chose to follow the call of their hearts. In a bold act of defiance, they fled, seeking refuge in the land and hoping to escape the consequences of their forbidden love. However, their tribe would not let them go so easily. As the lovers made their desperate escape, they were pursued relentlessly until, at last, they found themselves standing at the edge of the ocean with nowhere left to run.

It was in this moment of ultimate desperation that the young man turned to face his pursuers, throwing his spear in the hope that it would save them. His beloved fashioned more weapons from the sticks and stones at her feet, binding them together with strands of her hair. Together, they made their final stand, determined to protect their love at all costs.

But as their resources dwindled and with the angry tribespeople closing in, the lovers knew they faced a grim choice. They had to either surrender to a fate decreed by others or embrace the unknown depths of the ocean together. Clasping each other tightly, they chose the latter, stepping into the water. However, at that moment, when all seemed lost, the Great Spirit intervened. He was touched by the depth of their love and the courage of their defiance. The Great Spirit transformed the lovers into barramundi, granting them eternal life in the waters they had chosen as their escape.

Most barramundis are born male and eventually change to female, a mirror of the eternal bond between the man and woman, ensuring they would never be parted.

How the Cassowary Got Its Helmet

In Aboriginal culture, it is clear that the balance in the natural ecosystem is deeply respected, with each creature playing a vital role. However, the cassowary stands out as a leader and guardian of the rainforest. Cassowaries are recognized for their importance to the biodiversity of the Wet Tropics and Cape York. This majestic bird is also considered a prized food, with their feathers, claws, and bones valued for ornaments and tools.

Three species of cassowary.[46]

The story of how the cassowary got its helmet is a tale that portrays the bird's journey from an outcast to a respected member of the animal kingdom. It all began long ago in the lush, verdant expanses of the rainforest during a time when all beings lived in harmony. A young cassowary found himself the subject of relentless teasing due to his inability to fly. Isolated and saddened, he watched from the shadows as the other animals played in the water. He wanted to join, but he was worried about being teased.

One day, after the animals had left the swimming hole, the cassowary ventured out, hoping to enjoy a solitary swim and perhaps catch some fish for his dinner. However, his presence did not go unnoticed. A lizard spotted the cassowary hiding and called out to the others, mocking the bird for his flightlessness. The laughter that followed cut deep, and in his distress, the cassowary fled into the forest, crashing into a large rock with such force that a piece of stone became lodged in his head.

Embarrassed and hurt, the cassowary withdrew even further from the community, spending his days alone. One day, he encountered a seahawk, who offered him a new perspective.

"Hello there," the seahawk greeted the cassowary in a warm tone, surprising the bird. "What are you doing here all alone?"

"Well, I suppose being alone is better than being constantly teased by others," the cassowary replied. "They all make fun of my inability to fly, except you. I can't help but wonder why you're not teasing me like your friends do."

The seahawk smiled. He reassured the cassowary that he was different from the rest. He told the cassowary that everyone in this world has their own unique abilities and contributions. While the cassowary did not possess the ability to fly, he had other skills. The seahawk pointed out the cassowary's exceptional skills in fishing—the cassowary claimed he could easily catch fish in the river by spreading his wings, acting like a net—his talent for digging up yams with his claws, and, of course, his newfound strength that came with the stone helmet.

His moment of valor arrived the next day when the seahawk, injured by a group of attacking snakes, sought the cassowary's help. With courage fueled by his desire to protect his friend, the cassowary charged into the fray, using his powerful legs, sharp claws, and hard helmet to fend off the snakes.

From that day forth, the cassowary was no longer seen as a figure to mock. Instead, he was seen as a fearless leader and protector of the forest. The animals, who had once been quick to laugh, now looked at the cassowary with respect and gratitude, lifting him up as a hero.

This story, like many Dreamtime narratives, teaches the importance of recognizing and embracing one's unique qualities. It speaks to the importance of community, the strength found in diversity, and the role each being plays in maintaining the balance within the ecosystem.

To the Aboriginal people, natural elements are far more than resources for survival. They are imbued with spiritual significance, serving as totems that link individuals and communities to the land and its ancient stories. Rocks, rivers, plants, and animals are all honored as teachers and kin. A rock might embody the strength and endurance of the land, while a river may represent life's ever-flowing, ever-changing journey.

This holistic view of the world fosters a profound respect for the environment, teaching the importance of living in harmony with nature. It instills a sense of stewardship and a responsibility to care for the earth.

In Aboriginal cultures, every aspect of nature is a thread in the intricate web of life, each with its own story and significance. The natural world is a sacred space where the spiritual and physical realms merge.

Chapter 10: Spirits of the Outback

A lone man could be seen sitting by his campfire. It was dark, save for the glinting stars high up in the sky and the faint glow of the fire in front of him. Suddenly, his mind raced to the various stories he had heard about the Outback—the semi-arid inland areas of Australia that are typically remote—and the spirits that inhabited it. The man could feel his heart beating slightly faster as he recalled these stories, but he kept calm, reminding himself that they were nothing more than stories that served as warnings for wandering travelers like him to be cautious of their surroundings.

Indeed, it was just another calm night for the man until he heard an unsettling scraping sound breaking the stillness from somewhere nearby. His only reaction was to freeze; he dared not move a muscle. His gaze darted toward the dense line of trees where he thought the sound might have come from. His heart skipped a beat. Just beyond the reach of the firelight, the man saw a pair of eyes glinting with an unnatural glow. The figure emerged from the dark, its shadowed silhouette with long limbs immediately sending shivers down his spine.

The creature slowly approached, each of its steps making a rough, echoing scrape. This was because of its knees, which were encased in hard stone, knocked together as the creature walked. The man's terror grew as he saw a stone knife in one of the creature's hands. This sight confirmed his nightmare; the creature was none other than the Malingee.

According to Aboriginal mythology, Malingee is a rare and fearsome spirit that embodies the wild dangers of the night. The Malingee is especially familiar to the Aboriginal nations of the Northern Territory. The Malingee can be merciless when provoked, but it never seeks humans out for sport. It prefers to remain hidden, enjoying the silence of its domain. Yet, those who unwisely set up a campfire near its presence risk its wrath.

Interestingly, legend has it that the Malingee was not always a horrifying spirit of the night. Based on one version of the story, the spirit was once a man who wandered the land. Things changed when he crossed paths with a shaman. Details of this story are foggy, but the gist is that he somehow angered the shaman. As a punishment, he was transformed into a twisted creature, his humanity stripped away forever. There is no way to reverse the curse, and the man, now known as the Malingee, can only wander the Outback forever. He often hides within the dense forest or in caves, avoiding sunlight. Only when the sky turns dark does he emerge, occasionally targeting those who unconsciously disturb his domain.

Apart from the Malingee, the Outback is also the home of another spirit known as the Papinijuwari. Described as a giant with only a single eye, the Papinijuwari are believed to dwell in huts at the ends of the sky. This creature carries a torch whenever it sets out across the heavens. Its movement in the sky appears to human eyes as a shooting star.

In contrast to the Malingee, who do not typically seek humans, the Papinijuwari has an insatiable appetite. Drawn specifically to the scent of illness, the creature tracks down the sick. Once it has found its victim, the Papinijuwari drinks their blood. The terror does not stop there; the Papinijuwari then shrinks itself to a size small enough to enter the victim's body. Once inside, the spirit continues to feast, ultimately leading to the victim's death. Fortunately, sightings of Papinijuwari are rare. However, their presence is deeply feared—some might even consider the Papinijuwari to be one of the most dreaded spirits in Aboriginal folklore.

Moha Moha

Even the waters of Australia teem with mystery. The seas around the Great Barrier Reef hold their own collection of supernatural beings. One of them is named the Moha Moha.

Almost similar to the legend of the Loch Ness Monster, several sightings of Moha Moha have been reported. The first detailed account came from an unexpected witness in 1890, a schoolteacher named Selina Lovell. The encounter took place on the shores of Great Sandy Island. Here, Lovell claimed to have witnessed the creature from only five feet away. For nearly half an hour, the schoolteacher watched the Moha Moha as it lingered in the shallows. It then turned and raised its body and tail above the water, revealing itself to the human for a short while before it slipped back into deeper waters, disappearing as suddenly as it had appeared.

Lovell described the creature vividly. It was nearly thirty feet long and had a massive dome-shaped body. Its serpentine neck, extending toward a saurian head, made the creature appear rather unsettling. The Moha Moha also had glossy skin, as if it were made of satin, while its head and neck were greenish-white. White spots dotted along its neck, and around its inky black eyes were a stark white band. Lovell claimed the Moha Moha had no visible nostrils but had serrated teeth. Because of this, many have concluded that it breathed through its mouth.

Perhaps the most peculiar feature of the creature is its greyish dome-shaped carapace, which spanned at least eight feet across and five feet high. The Moha Moha also sports a twelve-foot tail covered entirely in thumb-sized scales and has a brownish fin. Its head and tail apparently look like they come from different animals; some may even say the Moha Moha is almost similar to the Greek mythological creature the Chimera, which had different parts of animals attached to its body.

While the sighting must have left a lasting impression on Lovell, the Aboriginal people, especially those who called these coasts their home, were not at all surprised upon learning of this sighting. The Aboriginals view the Moha Moha as a coastal spirit who emerges from the sea every once in a while. However, this spirit is far from benevolent; once on land, it attacks camps and seizes unsuspecting people by the leg. These tales are popular among the Aboriginal nations because they serve as a warning of the ocean's hidden dangers.

Believe it or not, Lovell was not the only person to have reported a sighting of the Moha Moha. Captain James Cook claimed to have caught a glimpse of the spirit during his 1770 voyage. In the 1960s, another sighting was reported. This time around, it was by a fisherman named Jacob Lack. Instead of witnessing the spirit in the flesh, the fisherman was said to have come across its carcass decomposing on a rock.

Nadubi and Garkain

The Nadubi is well known among those on the rocky plateaus of Arnhem Land. According to the natives, the Nadubi is a spirit that often emerges in the chilly hours of the night. Its target is lone wanderers. At a single glance, the Nadubi might look like a human, but as one gets closer, there are a few fearsome distinctions that will terrify even the bravest. The spirit is often seen haunting the rugged terrain with sharp, barbed spines protruding from its elbows.

Ancient cave paintings across Arnhem Land captured the appearance of this spirit in detail. The painting in Gunbalanya, for instance, depicts Nadubi as a woman with spines sprouting not only from her elbows but also her lower body. Another mural at Sleisbeck pictures the Nadubi in a different form; the spirit was painted as a kangaroo-like figure with a spiny tail and barbed spines coming out from its mouth.

Legend has it that after silently stalking lone travelers, the Nadubi will attack them by projecting its barbed spines. They are lethal. The unsuspecting victims feel a slow and agonizing sickness creeping in as the spines pierce their flesh. They will eventually die unless the spines are swiftly removed. However, removing them is not an easy feat, and not everyone can do it. Only medicine men possess the knowledge to save these victims. Apart from having the skills to remove the lethal spines, these medicine men are also believed to have been gifted with a special sight, allowing them to detect the Nadubi's presence. However, the removal has to be done quickly; there are a lot of cases where help arrives too late.

While the Nadubi haunts the rugged plateaus, somewhere near the mouth of the Liverpool River dwells another solitary spirit. Known simply as the Garkain, this mysterious spirit also appears vaguely human in appearance. His biggest distinction is the large flaps of skin on his arms and legs, appearing similar to wings or massive fins. Because of this special feature, the Garkain has the ability to fly. He prefers to remain hidden during the day—he typically rests in silence beneath piles of leaves—but when the sky darkens, the spirit wreaks havoc, attacking anyone who trespasses into his territory.

To eliminate his victim, the Garkain first launches the individual into the air before swooping down upon them. Using his leathery flaps of skin, the spirit then wraps around the unfortunate traveler. Through this method, the spirit can suffocate his victims. This, however, is not the end of the traveler. The Garkain feasts on his victim. Since the spirit is tied deeply to his primal instincts—not knowing how to make fire or use tools—the Garkain often eats these wandering travelers raw.

The Yara-ma-yha-who, a Vampire-Like Creature

The legend about the Yara-ma-yha-who is one of the popular tales told to keep little ones safe. Parents often warn their children to steer away from giant fig trees scattered throughout the landscape, as this is where the Yara-ma-yha-who is said to wait for its next victim.

According to legend, the Yara-ma-yha-who has a rather small appearance. The spirit has a large head and oversized mouth. Apart from being red in color, the Yara-ma-yha-who's most striking feature is its fingers that end in tiny suction pads.

Since it often sits perched on branches of fig trees, the spirit can easily camouflage itself with the leaves and the branches. It will wait for hours for an unsuspecting traveler or a child to wander close to the tree where it dwells. The moment an individual approaches the tree, either to take a quick rest or even to seek shade, the Yara-ma-yha-who immediately seizes its opportunity. The spirit drops down without warning, clinging to its victim with its suction-cup fingers. Its grip is believed to be so strong that escape is nearly impossible. Then, the Yara-ma-yha-who proceeds to drink the blood of its struggling victim. However, unlike a typical vampire, the spirit never drains its victim completely. Instead, it drinks just enough to weaken them.

The spirit will leave its victim alone as it continues to stroll around, working up its appetite. With no strength, victims often find it extremely difficult to walk, let alone attempt an escape. They are left with no choice but to remain on the ground, waiting for the return of the spirit. When that moment comes, the Yara-ma-yha-who opens its mouth wide, almost like a hungry python, and swallows its victim headfirst, forcing them down into its belly. Once its prey is completely swallowed, the spirit stands upright and performs a rhythmic dance as if celebrating the feast.

Surprisingly, the horror does not stop there. After filling itself up, the spirit lays down, eventually drifting into a slumber. When it wakes, the Yara-ma-yha-who spits its victim out. Although still alive, the victim is no longer themself. According to the Aboriginal storyteller and writer David Unaipon, after their first encounter with the Yara-ma-yha-who, victims will find themselves shorter and weaker, with a hint of redness to their skin. If these same victims are unfortunate enough to cross paths with the spirit for a second time, they will grow even shorter, and their features will turn increasingly distorted. A third encounter is the worst of all; victims will transform into a Yara-ma-yha-who, cursed to turn into the very spirit that had harmed them.

Bunyip

The bunyip is known by many names. The Dharawal people of Australia's southeastern coast refer to the spirit as gu-ru-ngaty; the Wiradjuri people call it mirree-ulla. The Wemba-Wemba people call it banib and describe it as a mysterious creature that dwells in the waters along the Dhungala, or the Murray River. However, bunyip remains the most common name used to refer to the spirit.

Descriptions of the spirit vary significantly among Aboriginal nations. Some claim it appears as a half-human, half-fish creature with sharp fangs. It is also thought to possess eerie, mystical powers and has a chilling appetite for human flesh, especially innocent children. A bunyip can also let out echoing cries that inflict fear. It is also said to carry diseases such as rheumatism. Some agree that the bunyip is a shapeshifter; at times, it appears covered in shaggy fur, while other times, it appears coated in shiny scales and feathers. The spirit can also take the form of a dog, a massive cow, a seal-like creature, or even an emu. The colonial explorer George French Angas claimed that the spirit resembled a massive starfish.

The bunyip's origin also remains a topic of debate. Renowned paleontologists such as Pat Vickers-Rich and geologists like Neil Archbold proposed an intriguing theory regarding the origin of the spirit. These professionals suggest that the origin of the spirit traces back to sightings of the now-extinct *Diprotodon*, a giant herbivorous marsupial that once roamed Australia in ancient times. Early Aboriginal Australians inhabited the region alongside megafauna like *Diprotodon* for about twenty thousand years before these creatures went extinct. It could be plausible that stories of the bunyip evolved from sightings of this ancient animal.

Meanwhile, the Ngarrindjeri people of southeastern Australia claim that the legend of the bunyip—referred to as Mulyawonk by them—is born from a story about greed. The tale begins with a man who was beyond famished. Consumed by both hunger and greed, he caught more fish than he needed, thus depleting resources for others. To punish the greedy man, the elders cursed him, transforming half of the man's body into a fish-like creature. To this day, the Ngarrindjeri never fail to express caution that overfishing or environmental exploitation could awaken the bunyip, bringing misfortune upon those who show no respect for nature's balance.

Of course, the intriguing tales and descriptions of the mysterious bunyip caught the attention of many, including the European settlers when they arrived in Australia in the 18th century. Their curiosity peaked in 1846 when the world was surprised by news of the discovery of a peculiar skull unearthed in a tributary of the Murray River. Believed to be the remains of a bunyip, the skull was exhibited at Sydney's Australian Museum. However, this excitement was short-lived. After a careful scientific investigation, scholars revealed that the skull belonged not to the legendary water spirit but to a deformed horse.

The Terrorizing Whowie

Similar to the bunyip, the Whowie also dwells in the Murray River, particularly in the Riverina district of Australia. Resembling a giant goanna, the Whowie measures about twenty feet long and has six powerful legs that look like those belonging to a monitor lizard. Its head, however, resembles a frog, which makes its entire appearance both strange and frightening.

Despite having six powerful legs, the Whowie's movement is considered slow and deliberate. However, the spirit has little need for speed since its presence alone can send anyone who stumbles upon it fleeing in terror. When night comes, the Whowie can often be seen crawling into camps, sneaking in while people are deep asleep. The spirit captures anyone who is slow to escape and devours them whole. The Whowie is believed to have a mouth so massive that it can consume sixty people at one time. It is only when the sun begins to appear on the horizon that the Whowie retreats back to its cave on the Murray River. At times, the spirit can be seen basking along the riverbanks; some believe that the sandy hills of the Riverina were formed by the movement of this enormous spirit.

According to a legend passed down by the Aboriginals, there was a time when the Whowie went on a rampage. Its relentless attacks took a serious toll on the water-rat tribe that lived along the river. As desperation and fear grew, the tribe's chief thought it was high time for him to gather his people and discuss their dire situation. The chief eventually suggested that they abandon their home and make their way to safer lands. The people were saddened by this suggestion.

Suddenly, an elder stepped forward. He reminded the people of all the bountiful resources that their land had gifted them and the deep connection they had to the land. "We cannot lose hope now," the elder said. "Let us take another moment to think of other ways to rid this menace from our land."

Inspired by the words of the elder, the tribe agreed to stand their ground and end the threat of the Whowie once and for all. The water-rat tribe began to strategize. First, they set up night guards to watch over the people. Then, they summoned nearby tribes for assistance, hoping that by working together, they could at least drive away the spirit. This call for arms was a success; tribes from all over the land, including the kangaroo, platypus, eagle, magpie, cockatoo, lizard, snake, opossum, and crow tribes, came to lend their strength. Together, the people held a great corroboree, where they spent the night dancing and telling stories. It was only when dawn came that they made a move to find the Whowie.

After following tracks and traces left behind by the Whowie, the people successfully found its lair; it was a cave with only a single entrance. The cave was believed to be so vast that it would take the Whowie nearly a week to crawl out. The people prepared their trap. They first gathered massive piles of sticks and branches before bundling them into heaps. They arranged the wood halfway inside the cave and at its entrance, creating a barricade of fuel for their fire.

After a while, scouts came back, reporting that the Whowie was about to emerge. With haste, they set the wood ablaze, causing thick smoke and flames to fill the cave. A roar pierced the air, as the Whowie found itself trapped inside its very own shelter. The spirit could do nothing; it was helpless against the choking smoke. It struggled through the narrow passages for six days. Blinded and suffocating from the thick smoke, the Whowie grew more and more desperate to reach the exit. It eventually reached the mouth of the cave on the seventh day, though it was barely alive; it was already burned and desperately gasping for air.

Seizing the opportunity, the tribes immediately launched their attack. With their spears, axes, and nulla-nullas (a type of hardwood club used by the Aborigines), they laid blows on the giant goanna. No longer able to defend itself, the Whowie, which was already mortally wounded, dragged itself back into the cave. The tribes never saw the spirit again.

However, many believe that the Whowie still remains in the cave. Its sigh can sometimes be heard from the cave on the Murray River. Although the giant lizard is no longer a threat to the tribes, his legend continues to be remembered and feared. Elders warn lone travelers of such a spirit in the wilds, and parents often warn their children with tales of the Whowie, urging them to behave unless they want the spirit to emerge from his cave and wreak terror once more.

Chapter 11: Aboriginal Warriors Who Fought for Their Lands

The year was 1783, and Britain had just lost its grip on its American colonies. The blow left the empire scrambling for solutions to new and pressing problems. In the wake of the American Revolutionary War, the jails of England swelled with inmates, a result of ending the practice of transporting convicts to the American colonies. Desperate for an alternative, the British government turned its eyes to a distant land that had already been claimed for the British Crown by James Cook: Australia.

A depiction of Cook's landing at Botany Bay, located in Sydney. [47]

The convicts destined for transportation were a diverse lot, with the majority of their crimes considered minor in today's justice systems. Many were guilty of petty theft, a crime often born out of necessity rather than malice. The majority of these convicts hailed from England's teeming industrial cities, showing the widespread poverty and desperation that plagued the lower classes. Another small portion came from Ireland, and an even smaller number hailed from Scotland and Wales.

The solution to England's overcrowded jails materialized in the form of the First Fleet. This was an armada of eleven ships commanded by Captain Arthur Phillip, a highly experienced British naval officer tasked with founding a penal colony in an uncharted territory. Under Phillip's leadership, the fleet eventually reached the shores of what is now known as Circular Quay. On January 26th, 1788, they established a convict settlement at Sydney Cove. This date marked the beginning of convict settlements in Australia, a monumental event that would forever change the trajectory of the land and its people.

Of course, setting up a new settlement was anything but a walk in the park. The colony immediately grappled with the threat of starvation. The seeds they had brought all the way from England either spoiled or failed to grow in the Australian soil. The weather was completely different, and the majority of people knew nothing about farming the land.

Captain Phillip knew he must do everything he could to ensure the survival of the colony. He first insisted that what little food there was had to be shared equally among convicts and free settlers. This decision, along with his policy of granting land to convicts he deemed trustworthy, drew ire from the British officers. Yet, these policies allowed the colony to survive.

The landing of the First Fleet in Port Jackson, 1788. *

However, despite their efforts to make the colony work, the British soon realized they faced another challenge, one that was far bigger than the struggles of establishing farms or managing dissent. The colonizers were about to meet the Aboriginal warriors, the original inhabitants and traditional custodians of the vast land. The warriors were strong fighters and determined to protect their homes.

So, now we turn our attention to Pemulwuy, an Aboriginal warrior whose bravery and fight against the foreign settlers marked a significant chapter in Australian history.

Pemulwuy: The Fearless Bidjigal Warrior

Pemulwuy's story begins in the heartland of the Bidjigal clan, which is part of the broader Eora nation that originally inhabited what is now known as Sydney. The British settlers were made aware of Pemulwuy's existence as early as October 1790, thanks to Bennelong, an Aboriginal man who had forged a relationship with the colonizers. Bennelong, who had been captured by Governor Arthur Phillip but later became an intermediary between the British and Aboriginal people, mentioned Pemulwuy to the foreigners. It is still uncertain whether Bennelong's intention was to warn the British about Pemulwuy specifically or if there were other reasons behind his mentioning the warrior. However, as an intermediary, it makes sense for Bennelong to share information about significant figures within the Aboriginal communities (by this time, Pemulwuy had already displayed signs of resistance against the British encroachment).

Pemulwuy was also known to be a *carradhy*, or a clever man, as he possessed abilities that went beyond the ordinary, including healing wounds. Colebee, a Cadigal headman, informed Governor Phillip that Pemulwuy could be easily recognized by an injury to the toes of his left foot, which had been caused by a club. This detail fascinated many, as anthropologists have observed similar customs among the kadaicha men of Central Australia (spiritual enforcers who carry out justice or punishments within the community according to traditional law), who would dislocate their small toes to move quickly and quietly. There were even stories that Pemulwuy could transform himself into a bird to flee from danger.

An illustration of Pemulwuy in his canoe. [40]

The first major conflict between Pemulwuy and the British occurred on December 10th, 1790, and involved the spearing of John McIntyre, Governor Phillip's gamekeeper. This incident was not just a random act of violence but also a calculated response to the tensions simmering between the Aboriginal people and the settlers. On that day, McIntyre was resting in a hide with a hunting party near Cooks River when they heard noises from the bush. Investigating the sounds, they saw four Aboriginal men, including Pemulwuy, stealthily approaching.

McIntyre believed he recognized the men and halted his party from attacking. He attempted to communicate with the Aboriginals, offering them bread as a gesture of peace. However, when he laid down his gun, Pemulwuy stepped onto a log, positioned his spear on his *woomera* (spear thrower), and launched it toward McIntyre. The spear, tipped with jagged silcrete flakes, struck McIntyre, piercing deep and perforating his lung. When the surgeon, John White, later removed the spearhead, he found it barbed with small pieces of red stone, a design meant to ensure it inflicted maximum damage.

Bennelong's Dual Loyalties

Upon the arrival of the British, the Eora people deliberately avoided contact. Governor Arthur Phillip was eager to understand the language and customs of the local population, so he resorted to a desperate measure: kidnapping. On November 25th, 1789, Bennelong and Colebee were captured as part of Phillip's plan. Once, Bennelong speared Phillip during a whale feast organized by the British to mend relations with the Eora. Despite this aggressive encounter, Phillip and Bennelong eventually reestablished their complicated relationship. Bennelong was even exposed to European culture and taken to England sometime in 1792. However, he returned to Australia three years later, only to find that his people were still experiencing even more hardship under British rule.

In hindsight, evidence suggests that Bennelong and Colebee might have indirectly collaborated with Pemulwuy in the spearing of John McIntyre. McIntyre was known for carrying a musket and competing with the Indigenous population for food. Bennelong deeply resented him. McIntyre trespassed on Bidjigal land, hunting animals that were considered totemic spirit ancestors by the local people, such as possums, kangaroos, emus, and dingoes. McIntyre was also suspected of having harmed or even killed several Aboriginal individuals during his hunting expeditions; some accounts even state that he admitted to shooting an Aboriginal man.

McIntyre survived the initial attack but succumbed to his wounds on January 20th, 1791. The incident shocked the settlement, as many believed the attack was unprovoked. After all, McIntyre had been unarmed at the time. Governor Phillip was convinced of the need for retribution and to assert control. He ordered a punitive expedition led by Captain Watkin Tench.

Perhaps consumed by his bloodthirst, Phillip demanded the capture of two Bidjigal men and ordered Tench to behead ten more. However, recognizing the brutality of such orders, Captain Watkin Tench proposed a less bloodthirsty plan. He suggested capturing six Bidjigal and bringing them to Sydney Cove, insisting that none should be killed outright. Phillip accepted Tench's proposal, and the expedition set out on December 14th, marking the largest military operation since the colony's founding. Despite their efforts, after three days of searching, there was no trace of Pemulwuy or the Bidjigal. On December 17th, Tench called for a retreat to Sydney Cove to regroup and resupply.

The resistance was just beginning, though. Pemulwuy persuaded the Eora, Dharug, and Tharawal people to join his campaign against the settlers. From 1792 onward, this formidable warrior led numerous raids on British colonists, striking at various sites and demonstrating his courage and strategic acumen.

In December 1795, Pemulwuy and his warriors launched an attack on a work party at Botany Bay, which included "Black Caesar," an early settler of African descent and a renowned bushranger (a term referring to outlaws in colonial Australia). Caesar managed to crack Pemulwuy's skull in the skirmish. Many believed this blow would be fatal, but Pemulwuy survived, cementing his legend and the belief in his near-immortality.

March 1797 saw Pemulwuy leading a daring raid against a government farm at Toongabbie. After a series of raids near Parramatta, a group of armed settlers and soldiers clashed with over one hundred Aboriginal warriors at dawn. The punitive party, tired of the chase, entered the town, only to be followed by Pemulwuy and a large group of warriors. Pemulwuy speared a soldier, sparking a battle. The settlers' first volley of gunfire killed at least five Aboriginal warriors. Pemulwuy was severely wounded, with seven buckshot wounds to his head and body.

Despite the severity of his injuries, Pemulwuy's capture did not spell the end of him. Held in custody at a Parramatta hospital, still filled with buckshot and shackled with a leg iron, he managed an astounding escape.

The Battle of Parramatta elevated Pemulwuy's stature among the Aboriginal people as an invincible figure. He was revered as the mastermind behind subsequent raids on British farms for food. However, his injuries limited his capabilities, leading to a diminished resistance effort in his final years.

On November 22nd, 1801, Governor Philip Gidley King issued a proclamation for Pemulwuy's capture, offering a reward for him, dead or alive. Then, in early June 1802, Pemulwuy's life came to an end at the hands of Henry Hacking, the first mate of the Royal Navy ship *Lady Nelson*.

Yet, the spirit and strength of the Aboriginal people did not end with Pemulwuy. Instead, his legacy ignited an even greater flame of resistance. Pemulwuy's son, Tedbury, took up his father's cause. He fought valiantly for several more years before his own death in 1810. Through their courageous efforts, the legacy of resistance and the indomitable spirit of the Aboriginal people lived on, proving their enduring fight for their land, culture, and rights.

Jandamarra: The Bunuba Resistance Leader

Born in the 1870s into the Bunuba tribe, Jandamarra's early years were marked by a unique bridging of worlds. The Bunuba people, known for their deep connection to the mountainous Kimberley region of Western Australia, faced the encroachment of European settlers with a mix of resistance and adaptation. At about the age of eleven, Jandamarra and his mother stepped away from the traditional life to settle at Lennard River Station, one of the earliest pastoral stations in the Kimberley. This decision marked the beginning of Jandamarra's complex relationship with the European world.

Under the expansive skies of the Kimberley and the watchful eyes of the settlers, Jandamarra quickly mastered skills that were alien to his people but essential for survival in a changing world. He became adept at riding horses, shearing sheep, and using firearms. His proficiency in these areas, coupled with his exceptional physical agility—despite his small stature, Jandamarra was swift—earned him the nickname "Pigeon" from William Lukin, the owner of the River Station. Jandamarra's ability to speak English fluently and confidently set him apart.

However, despite his early assimilation into station life, the call of his ancestral lands was strong. At the age of fifteen, Jandamarra returned to his traditional lands for initiation into Bunuba law, a rite of passage that reconnected him with his roots. He started to hone his hunting skills, blending his newfound talents with the traditional knowledge passed down through generations.

In 1889, a pivotal moment occurred when Jandamarra and a fellow tribesman—some said he was also Jandamarra's uncle—known as Ellemarra were captured by police at Windjina Gorge. They were accused of killing sheep. The two men were chained together and forced to march to Derby, where they were to be charged. After a period of incarceration, Jandamarra's charges were unexpectedly dropped. He was offered freedom in exchange for his services in caring for police horses.

About a year later, Jandamarra returned to Lennard River as a stockman. However, this was nothing more than a brief return. Perhaps hearing a whisper of calling from his ancestors, Jandamarra returned to his traditional land. He soon found himself in conflict with Bunuba law; since he worked for the settlers, he was seen as betraying his duty to protect his people's lands.

Hoping to avoid retribution, Jandamarra escaped and left his home yet again. Seeking refuge, he arrived at Lillimooloora Station, where fate introduced him to Bill Richardson, a stockman turned police officer. Richardson recognized Jandamarra's skills and, perhaps understanding the value of his knowledge of the land and people, employed him as a tracker. As an Aboriginal tracker, Jandamarra's duties were to assist the police in tracking down Aboriginal people who had a reputation for strongly resisting the settlers' encroachment on their land. Sometimes, these people were also tracked down simply for occupying or using land that settlers now claimed as their own. These targeted Aborigines often ended up getting removed from their land, never to be seen by their tribe or family again.

Together, Jandamarra and Richardson made a formidable team. They set a standard for effectiveness in tracking down those who sought refuge in the vast and rugged terrain of the Kimberley. Jandamarra and Richardson eventually developed a close relationship. There was also a time when Jandamarra saved Richardson's life from an assault launched by the Aborigines. However, this partnership put Jandamarra in a unique position. He was tracking down his own people, using the very skills that tied him to his culture and ancestors. Jandamarra navigated a delicate balance between survival and betrayal.

The work Jandamarra and Richardson undertook together was a source of deep inner turmoil for Jandamarra. He was torn between the loyalty he felt for his companion and the duty he owed to his people. Some sources claim that this period of Jandamarra's life was also marred by personal controversies. Allegations of reckless behavior, particularly in flouting kinship and skin laws, surfaced, complicating his standing within the Bunuba community.

However, Jandamarra soon realized that his ties with his people were stronger than he ever imagined. The settlers' livestock were frequently stolen or speared by Aboriginal people, a form of resistance against the invasion and the use of their lands. In response, the Europeans tasked Jandamarra with capturing a group of Bunuba men responsible for these actions at Lillimooloora Station. Upon successfully capturing the group, Jandamarra was immediately confronted with the reality of his actions. Among the captured group were not only the most senior Bunuba leaders and elders but also Ellemarra and a few of his own bloodline. They confronted Jandamarra.

"Look around you," Ellemarra said to him. "I raised you, yet look at what you have done to us."

Jandamarra felt a surge of guilt after being reminded of his obligations to his own people. The Bunuba also spoke of a new policeman at Fitzroy Crossing who had been recklessly killing Aboriginal people, further igniting Jandamarra's sense of duty to his community.

In a moment of defiance, Jandamarra shot and killed Richardson as he slept. He then armed his people, rallying a group of warriors to ambush the Europeans. On November 10th, 1894, this armed gang attacked five white men driving cattle through Bunuba land, killing two and seizing their weapons. This act of rebellion was a declaration of war against the European settlers and marked a significant escalation in the conflict.

The most famous battle under Jandamarra's leadership occurred in 1894 at Windjana Gorge. A fierce confrontation unfolded between fifty Bunuba warriors and thirty police officers. In the heat of battle, Ellemarra was killed, and Jandamarra was terribly wounded, yet he managed to escape. His miraculous recovery only added to his legendary status, instilling fear in the police across the state for his exceptional shooting skills and intimate knowledge of the land.

The growing retaliation led John Forrest, Western Australia's first premier, to order a crackdown on the rebellion. Police attacks on camps around Fitzroy Crossing resulted in the deaths of several Aboriginal people. They were killed purely on suspicion of having ties to Jandamarra's resistance band.

For the next three years, Jandamarra led a guerrilla war against the police and European settlers, employing hit-and-run tactics and vanishing acts that became the stuff of legends. One famous incident involved a police patrol tracking him to his hideout at Tunnel Creek's entrance, only for Jandamarra to disappear mysteriously through the tunnel system within the mountains.

Jandamarra's end came at the hands of another Aboriginal tracker, Micki or Minko Mick, who was reputed to possess magical powers. On April 1st, 1897, Mick tracked Jandamarra down and shot him dead at Tunnel Creek. The white troopers decapitated Jandamarra as proof of his demise, and his head was sent to a firearms company in England to showcase the "effectiveness" of their weapons. His family buried his body in the Napier Range, placing it inside a boab tree.

It has been over a century since his death, yet Jandamarra's legacy is still alive. His story is remembered in stories, dances, and songs, both traditional and contemporary. His legend was of a tragic hero caught between two worlds. Jandamarra's story was one of the most dramatic tales of the 19th-century conflict between Aboriginal people and white settlers, highlighting the complexities of identity, resistance, and the enduring spirit of the Aboriginal people.

Conclusion

We have journeyed across the expanse of Australia's heartlands, delved into the depths of its oldest stories, and discovered the wisdom of the world's most ancient natural wonders. These stories are not outdated tales. They are the voices of the ancestors, speaking of the creation, the land, and the laws that have guided Aboriginal peoples for tens of thousands of years. The importance of preserving these narratives cannot be overstated; they are a bridge to understanding the past, a guide for the present, and a legacy for the future.

Embedded within these tales are important moral lessons that resonate deeply with contemporary issues. Take, for instance, the story of Tiddalik the frog, who drank all the water in the world, causing a great drought. This tale warns of the dangers of greed and the importance of considering the needs of others, reflecting on our modern-day challenges of resource depletion and environmental sustainability. The legend of Gulaga Mountain teaches us about the deep connection between the land and life, reminding us of the nurturing role nature plays and our duty to protect and honor our natural world.

The stories of courageous fighters like Jandamarra and Pemulwuy, who resisted colonial forces to protect their land, revolve around the themes of resistance, resilience, and the fight for justice. These tales celebrate the heroic deeds of these figures and also underscore the value of standing up for one's rights and the protection of sacred lands.

By keeping these stories alive, we honor the legacy of those who have gone before us and offer a gift of knowledge and understanding to those who come after us. This is not just a responsibility that belongs to historians and scholars alone; it is a call to all of us to listen, learn, and share. Whether through books, storytelling, or digital media, efforts to preserve and share these stories are a step toward a richer, more connected world. It is about giving voice to the wisdom that has too often been overlooked yet has so much to offer in our search for a sustainable way to live on this planet.

Here's another book by Enthralling History that you might like

Free limited time bonus

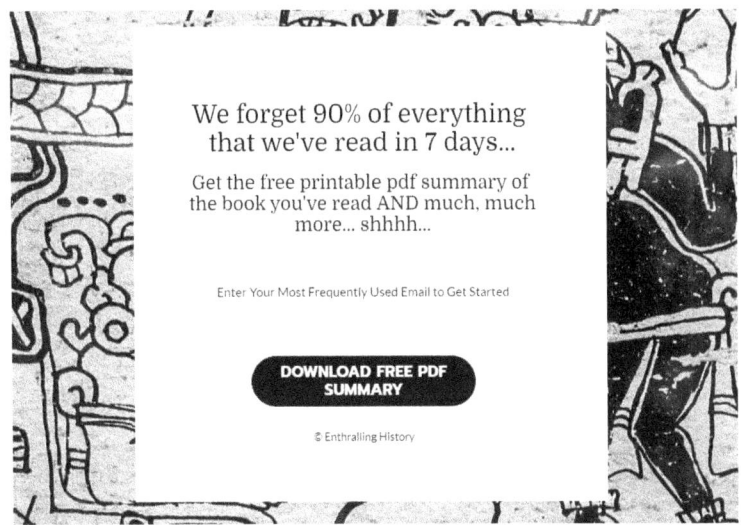

Stop for a moment. We have a free bonus set up for you. The problem is this: we forget 90% of everything that we read after 7 days. Crazy fact, right? Here's the solution: we've created a printable, 1-page pdf summary for this book that you're reading now. All you have to do to get your free pdf summary is to go to the following website:
https://livetolearn.lpages.co/enthrallinghistory/

Or, Scan the QR code!

Once you do, it will be intuitive. Enjoy, and thank you!

Further Reading and Reference

Part 1

Blainey, Geoffrey. *A Shorter History of Australia*. 1994.

Chambers, John H. *A Traveler's History of Australia*. 1999.

Clark, Manning. *A History of Australia*. 1988.

Docherty, J. C. *The A to Z of Australia*. 2010.

Grey, Jeffrey. *A Military History of Australia*. 1990.

Macintyre, Stuart. *A Concise History of Australia*. 1999.

Pahoff, Michael. *Australia: A New More Inclusive History*. 2021.

West, Barbara A. *A Brief History of Australia*. 2010.

Part 2

ABC News. (2018, August 18). My beloved Great Barrier Reef: Four tales of love, loss and hope. *ABC News*. https://amp.abc.net.au/article/9748398

Aboriginal belief and story. (n.d.). Flightless Birds. https://infoflightlessbirdshelp.weebly.com/aboriginal-belief-and-story.html

Australian Aboriginal Myths & Legends. (n.d.). https://members.optusnet.com.au/virgothomas/space/abobeliefs2.html

Bernheimer, K., Bernheimer, A., & Snøhetta. (2016). Fairy Tale Architecture: Tiddalik The Frog. *Places-a Forum of Environmental Design, 2016*. https://doi.org/10.22269/161219

Biography - Jandamarra - Indigenous Australia. (n.d.). https://ia.anu.edu.au/biography/jandamarra-8822

Bohra The Kangaroo. (n.d.). www.kullillaart.com.au. https://www.kullillaart.com.au/dreamtime-stories/Bohra-The-Kangaroo

Death and Sorry business | Common ground. (n.d.).
https://www.commonground.org.au/article/death-and-sorry-business

Dreamtime Stories: The Turtle. (2020, August 13). Yarn Marketplace.
https://www.yarn.com.au/blogs/yarn-in-the-community/dreamtime-stories-the-turtle

Dreamtime Story: The Seven Sisters. (2020, December 8). Yarn Marketplace.
https://www.yarn.com.au/blogs/yarn-in-the-community/dreamtime-story-the-seven-sisters

Gariwerd/Grampians - Budja Budja Aboriginal Cooperative. (2018, April 4). Budja Budja Aboriginal Cooperative.
https://budjabudjacoop.org.au/about/gariwerdgrampians/

Hamilton, J. (2020, October 7). Seven Sisters stars creation story reconnecting people to their country after clifftop massacre taboo lifted. *ABC News.*
https://www.abc.net.au/news/2020-10-08/wirangu-seven-sisters-songline-indigenous-healing-reconciliation/12380698

How the Sun was made. (n.d.). www.kullillaart.com.au.
https://www.kullillaart.com.au/dreamtime-stories/How-the-Sun-was-made

Japingka Aboriginal Art. (2022, January 31). *Rainbow Serpent Dreamtime Story - Japingka Aboriginal Art Gallery.* Japingka Aboriginal Art Gallery.
https://japingkaaboriginalart.com/articles/rainbow-serpent/#:~:text=Rainbow%20Serpent%20Rituals&text=They%20will%20sing%20out%20the,no%20harm%20or%20ill%20doing

Japingka Aboriginal Art. (2023, October 18). *Seven Sisters (Pleiades) star Dreaming Story - Aboriginal art stories.* Japingka Aboriginal Art Gallery.
https://japingkaaboriginalart.com/articles/star-dreaming-seven-sisters/

Kangaroo Totem and Dreamtime Stories. (2020, July 24). Yarn Marketplace.
https://www.yarn.com.au/blogs/yarn-in-the-community/kangaroo-totem-and-dreamtime-stories

National Theatre of Scotland. (2016, October 12). *Sharing a story through Aboriginal Australian Songline* [Video]. YouTube.
https://www.youtube.com/watch?v=QYziHh98AC8

Paul Taylor. (2015, March 12). *Gujingga Songline* [Video]. YouTube.
https://www.youtube.com/watch?v=oZGu7z2-XEU

Pemulwuy | The Dictionary of Sydney. (n.d.).
https://dictionaryofsydney.org/entry/pemulwuy

Reynolds, P. (n.d.). *An Anangu story.*
https://home.philreynolds.org.uk/travel/story.php

Songlines: Seven Sisters Tree Women and Wati Nyiru | The Box, Plymouth. (n.d.). The Box Plymouth. https://www.theboxplymouth.com/blog/art/songlines-tree-women

Stories in the stars. (n.d.). Museums Victoria. https://museumsvictoria.com.au/learning/little-science/teacher-support-materials/stories-in-the-stars/

Sydney Opera House. (2016, May 28). *Songlines explained: A 360 experience with Rhoda Roberts* [Video]. YouTube. https://www.youtube.com/watch?v=33O08xrQpR8

The birth of the Butterflies. (n.d.). www.kullillaart.com.au. https://www.kullillaart.com.au/dreamtime-stories/The-Birth-of-the-Butterflies

The First Fleet arrives at Sydney Cove | Australia's Defining Moments Digital Classroom | National Museum of Australia. (n.d.). https://digital-classroom.nma.gov.au/defining-moments/first-fleet-arrives-sydney-cove

The Guardian. (2019, December 7). *A healing corroboree at the foothills of Mount Gulaga, on Yuin country – in pictures.* https://www.theguardian.com/australia-news/gallery/2019/dec/08/a-healing-corroboree-at-the-foothills-of-mount-gulaga-on-yuin-country-in-pictures

The Lungkata story. (n.d.). Uluru-Kata Tjuta National Park. https://parksaustralia.gov.au/uluru/discover/culture/stories/lungkata-story/#:~:text=The%20western%20face%20of%20Uluru,traditional%20management%20of%20the%20land

The Rainbow Serpent | Common ground. (n.d.). https://www.commonground.org.au/bedtime-stories/the-rainbow-serpent

The Rainbow Serpent Dreamtime Story | Kate Owen Gallery. (n.d.). https://www.kateowengallery.com/page/rainbow-serpent#:~:text=Two%20brothers%2C%20known%20as%20the,Instead%2C%20he%20swallowed%20them%20whole

The Southern Cross. (n.d.). www.kullillaart.com.au. https://www.kullillaart.com.au/dreamtime-stories/The-Southern-Cross-Yaraan-doo-The-place-of-the-white-gum-tree

Vij, R. (2022, February 3). *Story from Australia: How the Kangaroo Got its Tail & Wombat its Flat-head?* NutSpace. https://nutspace.in/how-kangaroo-got-tail-wombat-flat-head/

Wikipedia contributors. (2024, February 13). *Australian Aboriginal religion and mythology.* Wikipedia. https://en.wikipedia.org/wiki/Australian_Aboriginal_religion_and_mythology#cite_note-FOOTNOTEBird_Rose2003163%E2%80%93168-34

Willis, L. (2022, February 2). *Returning to Country brings wellbeing.* Reconciliation Australia. https://www.reconciliation.org.au/returning-to-country-brings-wellbeing/

Image Sources

1. Thomas Schoch (= user Mosmas), CC BY-SA 3.0 <https://creativecommons.org/licenses/by-sa/3.0>, via Wikimedia Commons, https://commons.wikimedia.org/wiki/File:Aboriginal_Art_Australia.jpg
2. https://commons.wikimedia.org/wiki/File:Abel_Tasman_-_Cuyp_(cropped)_(adjusted).jpg
3. Lencer, CC BY-SA 3.0 <https://creativecommons.org/licenses/by-sa/3.0>, via Wikimedia Commons, https://commons.wikimedia.org/wiki/File:Australia_discoveries_by_Europeans_before_1813_en.png
4. https://commons.wikimedia.org/wiki/File:Captainjamescookportrait.jpg
5. https://commons.wikimedia.org/wiki/File:Arthur_Phillip_-_Wheatley_ML124.jpg
6. https://commons.wikimedia.org/wiki/File:Two_of_the_Natives_of_New_Holland,_Advancing_to_Combat.jpg
7. https://commons.wikimedia.org/wiki/File:Alexander_Schramm_-_A_scene_in_South_Australia_-_Google_Art_Project.jpg
8. https://commons.wikimedia.org/wiki/File:WilliamBligh.jpeg
9. https://commons.wikimedia.org/wiki/File:Mr_E.H._Hargraves,_The_Gold_Discoverer_of_Australia,_Feb_12th_1851_returning_the_salute_of_the_gold_miners_-_Thomas_Tyrwhitt_Balcombe.jpg
10. https://commons.wikimedia.org/wiki/File:Landing_at_melbourne_1840.jpg
11. https://commons.wikimedia.org/wiki/File:William_Strutt_Bushrangers.jpg
12. https://commons.wikimedia.org/wiki/File:Ned_Kelly_in_1880.png
13. https://commons.wikimedia.org/wiki/File:HenryParkes_Melbourne.jpg

14 https://commons.wikimedia.org/wiki/File:Australian_9th_and_10th_battalions_Egypt_December_1914_AWM_C02588.jpeg

15 https://commons.wikimedia.org/wiki/File:Menzies_Churchill_WW21941.jpg

16 https://commons.wikimedia.org/wiki/File:Aust_soldiers_Wewak_June_1945.jpg

17 https://commons.wikimedia.org/wiki/File:POWs_Burma_Thai_RR.jpg

18 https://commons.wikimedia.org/wiki/File:Melbourne-Punch-federation-Victoria-pest-Australian-Chinese-May-1888.jpg

19 State Library of New South Wales, No restrictions, via Wikimedia Commons, https://commons.wikimedia.org/wiki/File:Railway_Square,_ca._1945.jpg

20 https://commons.wikimedia.org/wiki/File:John_Howard_May_2006.jpg

21 ISAF Headquarters Public Affairs Office from Kabul, Afghanistan, CC BY 2.0 <https://creativecommons.org/licenses/by/2.0>, via Wikimedia Commons, https://commons.wikimedia.org/wiki/File:Australian_SOTG_wait_for_extraction_2011.jpg

22 NordNordWest, CC BY 3.0 <https://creativecommons.org/licenses/by/3.0>, via Wikimedia Commons: https://commons.wikimedia.org/wiki/File:Aboriginal_regions.png

23 Faithy05, CC BY-SA 3.0 <http://creativecommons.org/licenses/by-sa/3.0/>, via Wikimedia Commons: https://commons.wikimedia.org/wiki/File:Biamie%27s_Cave.jpg

24 Faithy05 at the English Wikipedia, CC BY-SA 3.0 <http://creativecommons.org/licenses/by-sa/3.0/>, via Wikimedia Commons: https://commons.wikimedia.org/wiki/File:Mt_Yengo.jpg

25 Ek2030372672, CC BY-SA 4.0 <https://creativecommons.org/licenses/by-sa/4.0>, via Wikimedia Commons: https://commons.wikimedia.org/wiki/File:ULURU.jpg

26 https://commons.wikimedia.org/wiki/File:Pleiades_Deep_dive.jpg

27 Starnutoditopo, CC BY-SA 4.0 <https://creativecommons.org/licenses/by-sa/4.0>, via Wikimedia Commons: https://commons.wikimedia.org/wiki/File:Seven_Sisters_coin_Royal_Australian_Mint_1_dollar_2020_Reverse.jpg

28 The original uploader was Digitaltribes at English Wikipedia., CC BY 2.5 <https://creativecommons.org/licenses/by/2.5>, via Wikimedia Commons: https://commons.wikimedia.org/wiki/File:RainbowSerpent.jpg

29 Nick-D, CC BY-SA 3.0 <https://creativecommons.org/licenses/by-sa/3.0>, via Wikimedia Commons: https://commons.wikimedia.org/wiki/File:Gosses_Bluff_crater_from_the_air_April_2014.jpg

30 Till Credner, CC BY-SA 3.0 <https://creativecommons.org/licenses/by-sa/3.0>, via Wikimedia Commons: https://commons.wikimedia.org/wiki/File:Constellation_Corona_Australis.jpg

31 Dylan O'Donnell, deography.com, CC0, via Wikimedia Commons: https://commons.wikimedia.org/wiki/File:M45_The_Pleiades_Seven_Sisters.jpg

32 Till Credner, CC BY-SA 3.0 <https://creativecommons.org/licenses/by-sa/3.0>, via Wikimedia Commons: https://commons.wikimedia.org/wiki/File:BootesCC.jpg

33 Till Credner, CC BY-SA 3.0 <https://creativecommons.org/licenses/by-sa/3.0>, via Wikimedia Commons: https://commons.wikimedia.org/wiki/File:Constellation_Crux.jpg

34 PotMart186, CC BY-SA 4.0 <https://creativecommons.org/licenses/by-sa/4.0>, via Wikimedia Commons: https://commons.wikimedia.org/wiki/File:Red_Kangaroos_at_Sturt_National_Park_NSW.jpg

35 PanBK at the English-language Wikipedia, CC BY-SA 3.0 <http://creativecommons.org/licenses/by-sa/3.0/>, via Wikimedia Commons: https://commons.wikimedia.org/wiki/File:Wombat-Narawntapu.jpg

36 Kpravin2, CC BY-SA 4.0 <https://creativecommons.org/licenses/by-sa/4.0>, via Wikimedia Commons: https://commons.wikimedia.org/wiki/File:Byron_Bay_Lighthouse,_Beach_and_Hinterland_in_the_Northern_Rivers,_NSW,_Australia.jpg

37 I, Thierry Caro, CC BY-SA 3.0 <http://creativecommons.org/licenses/by-sa/3.0/>, via Wikimedia Commons: https://commons.wikimedia.org/wiki/File:Eretmochelys-imbricata-K%C3%A9lonia-2.JPG

38 JJ Harrison (https://tiny.jjharrison.com.au/t/ZoQvcc05qhmjQ9eE), CC BY-SA 4.0 <https://creativecommons.org/licenses/by-sa/4.0>, via Wikimedia Commons: https://commons.wikimedia.org/wiki/File:Corvus_coronoides_-_Doughboy_Head.jpg

39 Ed Dunens, CC BY 2.0 <https://creativecommons.org/licenses/by/2.0>, via Wikimedia Commons: https://commons.wikimedia.org/wiki/File:Wedge-tailed_Eagle_(35713410886).jpg

40 JJ Harrison (https://www.jjharrison.com.au/), CC BY-SA 3.0 <https://creativecommons.org/licenses/by-sa/3.0>, via Wikimedia Commons: https://commons.wikimedia.org/wiki/File:Dacelo_novaeguineae_waterworks.jpg

41 en:User:Tnarg 12345, CC BY-SA 3.0 <http://creativecommons.org/licenses/by-sa/3.0/>, via Wikimedia Commons: https://commons.wikimedia.org/wiki/File:Cyclorana_platycephala.jpg

42 JJ Harrison (https://www.jjharrison.com.au/), CC BY-SA 3.0 <https://creativecommons.org/licenses/by-sa/3.0>, via Wikimedia Commons: https://commons.wikimedia.org/wiki/File:Tiliqua_scincoides_scincoides.jpg

43 Ayanadak123, CC BY-SA 4.0 <https://creativecommons.org/licenses/by-sa/4.0>, via Wikimedia Commons: https://commons.wikimedia.org/wiki/File:The_dazzling_colours_of_the_Great_Barrier_Reef_near_Airlie_Beach,_Whitsunday_Islands,_Queensland.jpg

44 https://commons.wikimedia.org/wiki/File:Bermagui_Beach_01.JPG

45 Mitch Ames, CC BY-SA 4.0 <https://creativecommons.org/licenses/by-sa/4.0>, via Wikimedia Commons: https://commons.wikimedia.org/wiki/File:Lates_calcarifer,_2014-09-19a.jpg

46 PaleoNeolitic (montage creator)BS Thurner HofKora27Martin Sordilla, CC BY-SA 3.0 <https://creativecommons.org/licenses/by-sa/3.0>, via Wikimedia Commons: https://commons.wikimedia.org/wiki/File:Cassowary_Diversity.jpg

47 https://commons.wikimedia.org/wiki/File:Cook%27s_landing_at_Botany_Bay.jpg

48 https://commons.wikimedia.org/wiki/File:The_First_Fleet_entering_Port_Jackson,_January_26,_1788,_drawn_1888_A9333001h.jpg

49 https://commons.wikimedia.org/wiki/File:Pemulwuy_aka_Pimbloy.jpg

www.ingramcontent.com/pod-product-compliance
Lightning Source LLC
Chambersburg PA
CBHW070327010526
44107CB00004B/448